ICT → INFORMATION COMMUNICATION TECHNOLOGY

DSR → DESIGN SCIENCE RESEARCH

GDC → GENERAL DESIGN CYCLE

Other Auerbach Publications in Software Development, Software Engineering, and Project Management

Accelerating Process Improvement Using Agile Techniques
Deb Jacobs
ISBN: 0-8493-3796-8

Advanced Server Virtualization: VMware and Microsoft Platforms in the Virtual Data Center
David Marshall, Wade A. Reynolds and Dave McCrory
ISBN: 0-8493-3931-6

Antipatterns: Identification, Refactoring, and Management
Phillip A. Laplante and Colin J. Neill
ISBN: 0-8493-2994-9

Applied Software Risk Management: A Guide for Software Project Managers
C. Ravindranath Pandian
ISBN: 0849305241

The Art of Software Modeling
Benjamin A. Lieberman
ISBN: 1-4200-4462-1

Building Software: A Practitioner's Guide
Nikhilesh Krishnamurthy and Amitabh Saran
ISBN: 0-8493-7303-4

Business Process Management Systems
James F. Chang
ISBN: 0-8493-2310-X

The Debugger's Handbook
J.F. DiMarzio
ISBN: 0-8493-8034-0

Effective Software Maintenance and Evolution: A Reuse-Based Approach
Stanislaw Jarzabek
ISBN: 0-8493-3592-2

Embedded Linux System Design and Development
P. Raghavan, Amol Lad and Sriram Neelakandan
ISBN: 0-8493-4058-6

Flexible Software Design: Systems Development for Changing Requirements
Bruce Johnson, Walter W. Woolfolk, Robert Miller and Cindy Johnson
ISBN: 0-8493-2650-8

Global Software Development Handbook
Raghvinder Sangwan, Matthew Bass, Neel Mullick, Daniel J. Paulish and Juergen Kazmeier
ISBN: 0-8493-9384-1

The Handbook of Mobile Middleware
Paolo Bellavista and Antonio Corradi
ISBN: 0-8493-3833-6

Implementing Electronic Document and Record Management Systems
Azad Adam
ISBN: 0-8493-8059-6

Process-Based Software Project Management
F. Alan Goodman
ISBN: 0-8493-7304-2

Service Oriented Enterprises
Setrag Khoshafian
ISBN: 0-8493-5360-2

Software Engineering Foundations: A Software Science Perspective
Yingxu Wang
ISBN: 0-8493-1931-5

Software Engineering Quality Practices
Ronald Kirk Kandt
ISBN: 0-8493-4633-9

Software Sizing, Estimation, and Risk Management
Daniel D. Galorath and Michael W. Evans
ISBN: 0-8493-3593-0

Software Specification and Design: An Engineering Approach
John C. Munson
ISBN: 0-8493-1992-7

Testing Code Security
Maura A. van der Linden
ISBN: 0-8493-9251-9

Six Sigma Software Development, Second Edition
Christine B. Tayntor
ISBN: 1-4200-4426-5

Successful Packaged Software Implementation
Christine B. Tayntor
ISBN: 0-8493-3410-1

UML for Developing Knowledge Management Systems
Anthony J. Rhem
ISBN: 0-8493-2723-7

X Internet: The Executable and Extendable Internet
Jessica Keyes
ISBN: 0-8493-0418-0

AUERBACH PUBLICATIONS

www.auerbach-publications.com
To Order Call:1-800-272-7737 • Fax: 1-800-374-3401
E-mail: orders@crcpress.com

Design Science Research Methods and Patterns
Innovating Information and Communication Technology

Vijay K. Vaishnavi

William Kuechler Jr.

Auerbach Publications
Taylor & Francis Group
Boca Raton   New York

Auerbach Publications is an imprint of the
Taylor & Francis Group, an **informa** business

Auerbach Publications
Taylor & Francis Group
6000 Broken Sound Parkway NW, Suite 300
Boca Raton, FL 33487-2742

© 2008 by Taylor & Francis Group, LLC
Auerbach is an imprint of Taylor & Francis Group, an Informa business

Library of Congress Cataloging-in-Publication Data

Vaishnavi, Vijay.
   Design science research methods and patterns : innovating information and communication technology / authors, Vijay K. Vaishnavi and William Kuechler Jr.
      p. cm.
   Includes bibliographical references and index.
   ISBN 978-1-4200-5932-8 (alk. paper)
   1. Information technology. 2. Information technology--Research. 3. System design. 4. Decision support systems. I. Kuechler, William. II. Title.

T58.5.V354 2007
004.072--dc22   2007015093

Visit the Taylor & Francis Web site at
http://www.taylorandfrancis.com

and the Auerbach Web site at
http://www.auerbach-publications.com

Dedication

To my family for their love and support

Vijay K. Vaishnavi

Contents

PART II: PATTERNS

[The prefix ^M indicates that the pattern is a meta-level pattern, applicable to multiple stages in the research process. Meta-level patterns are explained in more detail at the end of the section "The General Design Cycle Revisited" in Chapter 5.]

Preface

The need for this work became clear during the first author's teaching of a research seminar course on design science research offered to doctoral students at Georgia State University over the past decade. The course focuses on research whose purpose is the improvement or innovation of ICT (information and communication technology) artifacts. This type of "improvement research" is identical in technique and philosophy to that conducted by numerous other research communities, including engineering and computer science, and yet we still have to find good published material that can be used for teaching students this type of research. Herbert Simon's book, *Sciences of the Artificial*, is a seminal work that has helped in realizing the uniqueness and importance of this type of research. The book, however, does not provide much guidance on how to perform this type of research.

A unique feature of this book is the use of *patterns* to present how to conduct design science research. The decision to use patterns to organize the knowledge presented here is based on our interest in patterns, the belief that patterns are an excellent mechanism for organizing and transmitting this type of knowledge, and the second author's positive experience with patterns during more than 20 years of ICT system design experience in industry. We firmly believe that over time we can find a set of patterns that can both communicate the goals and philosophy of design science research as well as provide firm direction to a researcher new to the discipline. In time, experienced design science researchers will hopefully also find this a useful explication and codification of some of the techniques they have used. We trust that the patterns presented here are a good start in this direction.

The ideas presented in this work have been shaped and influenced by the students in the research seminar course that the first author has taught. We would like to particularly mention the students in the 1996 offering of the course: Paul Cule, Gayle Dixon-Randall, David Gefen, Rich Klein, Bill Kuechler, Lynette Kvasney, George Littlejohn, and Linda Wallace; and the 1998 offering of the course: Ashley Bush, Gordon Depledge, Huoy Khoo, David Kuechler, Alisha Malloy, Amrit Tiwana, Rustam Vahidov, and Jie Yin. We would like to acknowledge their contributions to the patterns in this work and would like to thank them for their patience in learning the research process and tools through a systematic search for the desired knowledge. We would like to particularly acknowledge the contributions of the 1998 class to the patterns presented in this work. We are sure this work will be further improved by the contributions made by the current and future classes taking this course. While acknowledging the contributions to this work from the design science research seminar students, we take responsibility for all errors or omissions.

The book can be used as a text or a reference for any course in the ICT fields that deals with the conduct of research, in particular design science research. Thus, the book can be used at the doctoral level, masters level, and senior undergraduate level in the ICT fields that include information systems, information sciences, information technology, and computer science. The book will also be useful for students conducting research in engineering fields.

Vijay K. Vaishnavi
William Kuechler Jr.

About the Authors

Vijay K. Vaishnavi is Board of Advisors Professor of Computer Information Systems at Robinson College of Business, Georgia State University. He holds a Ph.D. from the Indian Institute of Technology, Kanpur, and has conducted postdoctoral work at McMaster University, Canada. His research covers several areas, including process knowledge management, semantic interoperability and information integration, virtual communities and directory services, inter-organizational coordination, object modeling and design, and data structures. He has authored numerous research papers in these and related areas. The National Science Foundation and private organizations including IBM, Nortel, and AT&T have supported his research. His papers have appeared in *IEEE Transactions on Software Engineering, IEEE Transactions on Knowledge and Data Engineering, IEEE Transactions on Computers, SIAM Journal on Computing, Journal of Algorithms, Decision Support Systems*, and several other major international journals and conference proceedings. Dr. Vaishnavi is an IEEE Fellow, and a member of the IEEE Computer Society, the ACM, and the AIS.

William Kuechler Jr. is an associate professor of Information Systems at the University of Nevada, Reno. He holds a B.S. in Electrical Engineering from Drexel University, and a Ph.D. in Computer Information Systems from Georgia State University. His two primary research themes are the cognitive bases of IS use, development, and education, and inter-organizational workflow and coordination. He has published in *MIS Quarterly, Communications of the ACM, IEEE Transactions on Knowledge and Data Engineering, Decision Support Systems, Journal of Electronic Commerce Research, IEEE Transactions on Professional Communications, Information Systems Management, Information Technology and Management, Journal of Information Systems Education,* the proceedings of WITS, HICSS, and other international conferences and journals. Dr. Kuechler is a member of the AIS and ACM.

Chapter 1

Introduction

Until recently many researchers considered it impossible to *teach* research, at least in the same way that less complex skills such as reading or basic mathematics can be taught. This is because the practice of research is a complex activity requiring the extended use of several poorly understood cognitive activities such as creativity and intuition; research is, at best, a semi-structured activity. There are no algorithmic "recipes" for performing research, and even the methodologies for research sometimes presented (including those in this book) are guidelines at best.

In the past, those wishing to become researchers were expected to serve an apprenticeship, frequently by way of graduate study at a university, usually under the close tutelage of a senior researcher in the field. During the course of the apprenticeship, which extended over a period of years, the student researcher would gradually become "socialized" to the paradigmatic community in which they worked. If successful, the student was inculcated with an intimate and frequently tacit (that is, internalized and largely unstated) understanding of the research field, including:

- The important research questions
- The research methods that the community considers legitimate for exploring the research questions
- The prior research that provided the grounding of the field
- Knowledgeable colleagues
- Acceptable outlets for the research, including journals and conferences

This method of training researchers is still the dominant practice in many fields of research that are considered "paradigmatic" — areas that typically have a significant history (such as the hard sciences) and a dominant set of research questions, methods for exploring them, and outlets for disseminating new knowledge. In contrast, information systems, along with many other disciplines centered on information and communication technology (ICT), are currently multi-paradigmatic; they draw research questions, methodologies, and grounding philosophies from multiple fields that are loosely united under a common interest in *understanding the way in which human-computer systems are developed, produce and process information, and influence the organizations in which they are embedded.* This book refers to these fields henceforward as ICT (information and communication technology) fields or disciplines.

It is because ICT is multi-paradigmatic that we felt the need to write this book. We believe researchers in ICT fields need a thorough grounding in each of the variety of research philosophies and techniques practiced in their field, and it simply is not practical for any student to undertake a multi-year apprenticeship in each of the major ICT research paradigms. Moreover, design science research as practiced in ICT fields is significantly different from the design-based research practiced in other fields (such as architecture or industrial design); the need for and manner of validation of research results, for example, is more emphasized in information systems (IS), human-computer interface (HCI), and many branches of software engineering due to the grounding of those fields in management science, psychology, and other statistically based descriptive disciplines.

The reason that design science research is applicable to ICT is due to some of the types of research questions that occur naturally in the field. Human-computer information producing and processing systems are, by their nature, complex and grounded in multiple disciplines. Questions frequently arise that have a sparse or nonexistent theoretical background, and exploring these is where design science research — exploring by building — excels. Cultures at all technological levels have always had the ability to build artifacts that produce useful results without fully understanding how the artifacts work or without being able to elucidate the principles that contribute to the making of good (or better) examples of the artifacts. Bridges, boats, and waterwheels are just three examples of important artifacts that were produced, used, and highly valued thousands of years before the physical principles underlying them were understood in a manner that enabled methodical, consistent performance improvement. In our culture, information systems are frequently constructed and used in a similar information vacuum: they do some useful work but no one is really sure how to make them better; they have significant effects on people and organizations, many unanticipated, and most poorly understood. Some schools of thought "instinctively" veer away from questions that lack a developed theoretical base to direct their experimentation. Design science research, on the other hand, thrives in just the sort of theoretical *terra incognita* that many areas of ICT still remain.

Another reason that emboldened us to write this book is that we felt the technique of the use of patterns — a formalized way of recording experience — would enable the written — as opposed to the verbal and imitative — communication of at least some of the concepts, techniques, and their subtle interrelationships that make up research praxis. Tutorials on research in any field are rare, and the use of *patterns* in such a tutorial is unique as far as we know. However, the use of patterns to communicate contextually rich information will be familiar to many ICT fields, including software and computer engineering.

This book is structured as follows. Chapter 2 provides an introduction to design science research (DSR) in ICT that describes DSR in relation to other information systems (IS) research paradigms with a longer history, such as positivist and interpretivist research. IS is the specific ICT field of the authors but the discussion is immediately applicable to ICT fields in general. Chapter 2 also relates DSR in ICT to DSR as practiced in other areas of intellectual exploration where it has a much longer history. A primary contribution of the chapter is the introduction of the *design research cycle*, which is developed as the universal method for the practice of DSR. At the beginning of the "Patterns" section (Part II) of the book, this method is presented as a "roadmap" for the use of the patterns presented in the actual practice of DSR.

Chapter 3 places DSR in the historical context of ICT systems research and ICT artifact development and refinement. The design research cycle is abstracted to become a framework for understanding the progress of entire fields of technological research and development over extended periods of time. The intent of Chapters 1 and 2 is to give readers an overview of and "feel for" DSR even if the paradigm is unfamiliar to them. Those coming to ICT research from management science or other business backgrounds will find much of the material on DSR new and we urge them to read the introductory chapters carefully before proceeding to Part II. Those from a technical background such as engineering or physical science* will see many similarities to these areas of investigation, but will also, on careful reading, note significant differences between DSR as practiced in ICT and in other fields.

Part II of the book contains the patterns themselves. At the beginning of this section is a short chapter (Chapter 5) on "Using Patterns to Illuminate Research Practice." It begins by introducing patterns as they are used in this book. The qualifier "as used in this book" is necessary because, although patterns are used in many fields for many purposes, a precise general definition has proven elusive. The chapter then draws on concepts from the introductory chapters and outlines a methodology for the practice of DSR that is keyed to the patterns presented in the remainder of the book. The patterns are grouped by chapter, with each chapter being applicable to one or more phases of the research methodology.

The book concludes with Part III, in which examples of published design science research, including some widely cited papers, are elaborated in terms of the patterns used (or could have been used) in the research program.

---

* Other fields, such as Education, also utilize DSR (DSSE, 1997), however, in practice, few students with a background in education proceed on to graduate work in ICT fields.

The authors have practiced design science research in the ICT fields of information systems and computer science for much of their careers and have found it rewarding both as an intellectual practice and in terms of the research results obtained. Although this is not the place for an extended discussion of the history of ICT research, we feel safe in saying that the field is dynamic, multi-paradigmatic, and IS in particular generates much current *design science research* discussion as it transitions from a managerial to a technological focus (Iivari, 2003). It is in the exploration of the technology of information and communications systems, better understanding of how information systems do what they do, and how to improve their performance even in the absence of a strong theoretical grounding that DSR is the paradigm of choice.

The book can be used as a general book, a textbook, or a reference book on design science research in ICT. As a general book, we recommend reading the first part of the book, followed by a quick review of the remainder of the book. As a textbook, we recommend reading the entire book and the actual use of patterns (Part II and Part III of the book) in carrying out a research project. As a reference book, we recommend reading the first part of the book, getting familiarity with the remainder of the book, and then using the patterns on an as-needed basis.

References

DSSE (1997). Special Issue of Design Studies on Design Education, *Design Studies*, 18(3), pp. 319–320.

Iivari, J. (2003). The IS CORE VII: Towards Information Systems as a Science of Meta-Artifacts. *Communication of the AIS*, 12 (October), Article 37.

1

DESIGN SCIENCE
RESEARCH
METHODOLOGY

Chapter 2

Introduction to Design Science Research in Information and Communication Technology*

Overview of Design Science Research

Research

Drawing heavily from Kuhn (1996; first published in 1962) and Lakatos (1978), research can be very generally defined as an *activity* that contributes to the *understanding* of a *phenomenon*. In the case of design science research, all or part of the phenomenon may be **created** as opposed to naturally occurring. The *phenomenon* is typically a *set of behaviors of some entity*(ies) that is found *interesting* by the researcher or by a group — a research community. *Understanding* in most Western research communities is *knowledge that allows prediction* of the behavior of some aspect of

---

* Adapted from the ISWorld design research page developed and edited by the authors at: http://www.isworld.org/Researchdesign/drisISworld.htm.

the phenomenon. The set of activities a research community considers appropriate to the production of understanding (knowledge) constitutes its research methods or techniques. Historically, some research communities have been observed to have nearly universal agreement on the phenomenon of interest and the research methods for investigating it; in this book we term these "paradigmatic" communities. Other research communities are bound into a nominal community by overlap in sets of phenomena of interest or overlap in methods of investigation. We term these "pre-paradigmatic" or "multi-paradigmatic" research communities. As of the writing of this book, *information systems* provides an excellent example of a multi-paradigmatic community.

Design

Design means "to invent and bring into being" [*Webster's Dictionary and Thesaurus*, 1992]. Thus, design deals with creating something new that does not exist in nature. The design of artifacts is an activity that has been carried out for centuries. This activity is also what distinguishes the professions from the sciences. "Schools of architecture, business, education, law, and medicine, are all centrally concerned with the process of design" (Simon, 1996; first published in 1969). However, in this century, natural sciences almost drove out the design from professional school curricula in all professions, including business, with exceptions for management science, computer science, and chemical engineering — an activity that peaked two or three decades after the World War II (Simon, 1996).

Simon sets out a prescription for schools of business and engineering (in which most information and communication technology (ICT) departments are housed) that has motivated this book to a considerable degree: "…The professional schools will reassume their…responsibilities just to the degree that they can discover a science of design, a body of intellectually tough, analytic, partly formalizable, partly empirical teachable doctrine about the design process …"

To bring the design activity into focus at an intellectual level, Simon (1996) makes a clear distinction between "natural science" and "science of the artificial" (also known as design science):

> A *natural science* is a body of knowledge about some class of things
> — objects or phenomena — in the world (nature or society) that
> describes and explains how they behave and interact with each other.
> A *science of the artificial*, on the other hand, is a body of knowledge
> about artificial (man made) objects and phenomena designed to meet
> certain desired goals.

Simon further frames sciences of the artificial in terms of an *inner environment*, an *outer environment*, and the *interface* between the two that meets certain desired goals. The outer environment is the total set of external forces and effects that act on the artifact. The inner environment is the set of components that make up the artifact and their relationships — the organization — of the artifact. The behavior of the artifact is constrained by both its organization and its outer environment. The bringing-to-be of an artifact, components, and their organization, which interfaces in a desired manner with its outer environment, is the design activity. The artifact is "structurally coupled" to its environment, and many of the concepts of structural coupling that Varela (1988) and Maturana and Varela (1987) have developed for biological entities are applicable to designed artifacts.

In a perspective analogous to considering design as the crafting of an interface between inner and outer environments, design can be thought of as a mapping from function space — a functional requirement constituting a point in this multidimensional space — to attribute space, where an artifact satisfying the mapping constitutes a point in that space (Takeda et al., 1990). Design, then, is knowledge in the form of techniques and methods for performing this mapping — the know-how for implementing an artifact that satisfies a set of functional requirements.

Can Design Be Research?

The question this chapter intends to answer in the affirmative is: can design (i.e., artifact construction) ever be considered an appropriate technique for conducting research in ICT fields? The question may seem strange to computer science and some other ICT fields where artifact construction is an integral part of the community paradigm. However, for information systems (IS), which is the academic community of this book's authors, artifact construction has only recently gained some legitimacy. The reason for this is the emergence of IS from management science, a positivist, empiricist community, less than 30 years ago. However, even artifact-based ICT fields can greatly benefit from the chapter's discussion of the "natural sciences bias," which tends to be dismissive of any research approach other than empirical experimentation in the furtherance of understanding natural phenomena. We pursue the question — can design be research — in the specific context of ICT in the next section. The remainder of this section discusses the question in the abstract using as exemplars communities other than ICT where the question of whether or not design is a valid research technique has for many years been a resounding "Yes."

Owen (1997) discusses the relation of design to research with reference to a conceptual map of disciplines (Figure 2.1) with two axes: Symbolic/Real and Analytic/Synthetic. The horizontal axis of the map position disciplines according to their defining activities: disciplines on the left side of the map are more concerned with exploration and *discovery*. Disciplines on the right side of the map are characterized more by invention and *making*. The map's vertical division (the symbolic/real axis) characterizes the nature of the subjects of interest to the disciplines — the

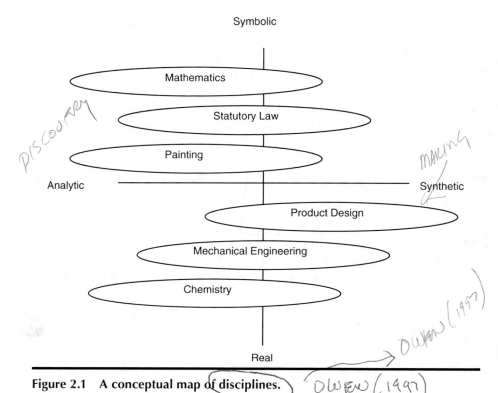

Figure 2.1 A conceptual map of disciplines. OWEN (1997)

nature of the phenomena that concerns the research community. Both axes are continua, and no discipline is exclusively concerned with synthesis to the exclusion of analytic activities. Likewise, no activity is exclusively concerned with the real to the exclusion of the symbolic, although the strong contrast along this axis between the physical science of chemistry (real) and the abstract discipline of mathematics (symbolic) is strongly and accurately indicated in the diagram.

The disciplines that lie predominantly on the synthetic side of the map are either design disciplines or the design components of multi-paradigmatic disciplines. Design disciplines have a long history of building their knowledge base through making — the construction of artifacts and the evaluation of artifact performance following construction. Architecture is a strongly construction-oriented discipline with a history extending over thousands of years. The architectural knowledge base consists of a pool of structural designs that effectively encourage the wide variety of human activities and has been accumulated largely through the post-hoc observation of successful constructions (Alexander, 1964). Aeronautical engineering provides a more recent example. From the Montigolfer balloon through World War I, the aeronautical engineering knowledge base was built almost exclusively by analyzing the results of intuitively guided designs — experimentation at essentially full scale.

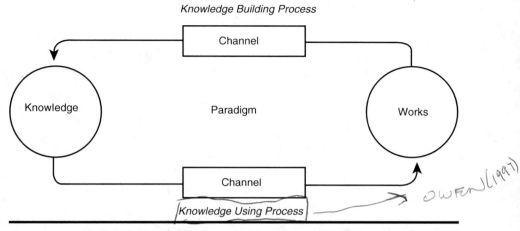

Figure 2.2   A general model for generating and accumulating knowledge.

Owen (1997) further presents a general model for generating and accumulating knowledge (Figure 2.2) that is helpful in understanding design disciplines and the design science research process: "Knowledge is generated and accumulated through action. Doing something and judging the results is the general model … the process is shown as a cycle in which knowledge is used to create works, and works are evaluated to build knowledge." While knowledge building through construction is sometimes considered to lack rigor, the process is not unstructured. The *channels* in the diagram of the general model are the "systems of conventions and rules under which the discipline operates." They embody the measures and values that have been empirically developed as "ways of knowing" as the discipline has matured. They may borrow from or emulate aspects of other discipline's channels but, in the end, they are special to the discipline and are products of its evolution."

Takeda et al. (1990) have analyzed the reasoning that occurs in the course of a general design cycle (GDC) illustrated in Figure 2.3. One can interpret this diagram as an elaboration of the "Knowledge Using Process" arrow in Figure 2.2. In following the flow of creative effort through this diagram, the types of new knowledge that arise from design activities and the reason that this knowledge is most readily found during a design effort will become apparent.

In this model, all design begins with *Awareness of a Problem.* Design science research is sometimes called "improvement research," and this designation emphasizes the problem-solving or performance-improving nature of the activity. *Suggestions* for a problem solution are abductively drawn from the existing knowledge or theory base for the problem area (Pierce, 1931). An attempt at implementing an artifact according to the suggested solution is performed next. This stage is shown as *Development* in Figure 2.3. Partially or fully successful implementations are then *Evaluated* (according to the functional specification implicit or explicit in the suggestion). *Development, Evaluation,* and further *Suggestions* are often iteratively

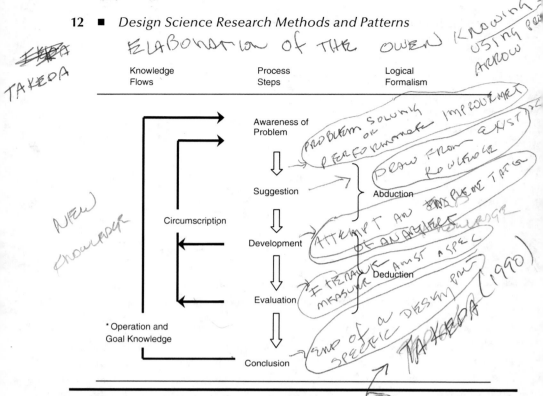

Figure 2.3   Reasoning in the general design cycle (GDC). (*An operational principle can be defined as "any technique or frame of reference about a class of artifacts or its characteristics that facilitates creation, manipulation and modification of artifactual forms" (Dasgupta, 1996; Purao, 2002).)

performed in the course of the research (design) effort. The basis of the iteration, the flow from partial completion of the cycle back to *Awareness of Problem,* is indicated by the *Circumscription* arrow. *Conclusion* indicates termination of a specific design project.

New knowledge production is indicated in Figure 2.3 by the arrows labeled *Circumscription* and *Operation and Goal Knowledge.* The *Circumscription* process is especially important in understanding design science research because it generates understanding that could only be gained from the specific act of construction. Circumscription is a formal logical method (McCarthy, 1980) that assumes that every fragment of knowledge is valid only in certain situations. Further, the applicability of knowledge can only be determined through the detection and analysis of contradictions — in common language, the design science researcher *learns or discovers* when things *do not* work "according to theory." This happens many times — not due to a misunderstanding of the theory, but due to the necessarily incomplete nature of *any* knowledge base. The design process, when interrupted and forced back to *Awareness of Problem* in this way, contributes valuable *constraint knowledge* to the understanding of the always-incomplete-theories that abductively motivated the original design.

The Outputs of Design Science Research

Even within design science research communities there is lack of consensus as to the precise objective — and therefore the desired outputs — of design science research. This book presents a broad perspective that explicates the types and levels of knowledge that *can* be derived from design science research while reserving judgment on whether a narrower goal of design science research should be held within any specific research community.

March and Smith (1995), in a widely cited paper contrasting design science research with natural science research, propose four general outputs for design science research: (1) constructs, (2) models, (3) methods, and (4) instantiations. *Constructs* are the conceptual vocabulary of a problem/solution domain. Constructs arise during the conceptualization of the problem and are refined throughout the design cycle. Because a working design (artifact) consists of a large number of entities and their relationships, the construct set for a design science research experiment may be larger than the equivalent set for a descriptive (empirical) experiment.

A *model* is "a set of propositions or statements expressing relationships among constructs." March and Smith identify models with *problem and solution statements*. They are proposals for how things are. Models differ from natural science theories, primarily in intent: natural science has a traditional focus on truth, whereas design science research focuses more on (situated) utility. Thus, a model is presented in terms of what it does and a theory described in terms of construct relationships. However, a theory can always be extrapolated to what can be done with the implicit knowledge, and a set of entities and proposed relationships can always be expressed as a theoretical statement of how or why the output occurs.

A *method* is a set of steps (an algorithm or guideline) used to perform a task. "Methods are goal directed plans for manipulating constructs so that the solution statement model is realized." Implicit in a design science research method then is the problem and solution statement expressed in the construct vocabulary. In contrast to natural science research, a method may well be the object of the research program in design science research. Because the axiology of design science research (see Table 2.3) stresses problem solving, a more effective way of accomplishing an end result — even or sometimes especially a familiar or previously achieved end result — is valued.

The final output from a design science research effort in March and Smith's explication is an *instantiation* that "operationalizes constructs, models, and methods." It is the realization of the artifact in an environment. Emphasizing the proactive nature of design science research, they point out that an instantiation sometimes precedes a complete articulation of the conceptual vocabulary and the models (or theories) that it embodies. We emphasize this further by referring to the aeronautical engineering example given previously: aircraft flew decades before a full understanding of how such flight was accomplished. And, it is unlikely the understanding would ever have occurred in the absence of the working artifacts.

Rossi and Sein (2003) and Purao (2002) in an ongoing collaborative effort to promote design science research in the IS community have set forth their own list of design science research outputs. All but one of these can be mapped directly to March and Smith's list. Their fifth output, *better theories*, is highly significant and merits inclusion in our general list of design science research outputs. Design science research can contribute to better theories (or theory building) in at least two distinct ways, both of which can be interpreted as analogous to experimental scientific investigation in the natural science sense. First, because the methodological construction of an artifact is an object of theorizing for many communities (e.g., how to build more maintainable software), the construction phase of a design science research effort can be an experimental proof of method or an experimental exploration of method, or both.

Second, the artifact can expose relationships between its elements. It is tautological to say that an artifact functions as it does because the relationships between its elements enable certain behaviors and constrain others. However, if the relationships between artifact (or system) elements are less than fully understood and if the relationship is made more visible than previously during either the construction or evaluation phase of the artifact, then the understanding of the elements has been increased, potentially falsifying or elaborating on previously theorized relationships. (Theoretical relationships enter the design effort during the abductive reasoning phase of Figure 2.3). For some types of research, artifact construction is highly valued precisely for its contribution to theory. Human-computer interface (HCI) researchers Carroll and Kellogg (1989) state that "…HCI artifacts themselves are perhaps the most effective medium for theory development in HCI." Walls et al. (1992) elaborate the theory-building potential of design and construction in the specific context of IS; however, their discussion is immediately applicable to all ICT fields. Table 2.1 summarizes the outputs that can be obtained from a design science research effort.

A different perspective on the output of design science research is developed in Purao (2002) following Gregg et al. (2001). In Figure 2.4, the multiple outputs of design science research are classified by level of abstraction.

Table 2.1　The Outputs of Design Science Research

	Output	Description
1	Constructs	The conceptual vocabulary of a domain
2	Models	A set of propositions or statements expressing relationships between constructs
3	Methods	A set of steps used to perform a task — how-to knowledge
4	Instantiations	The operationalization of constructs, models, and methods
5	Better theories	Artifact construction as analogous to experimental natural science

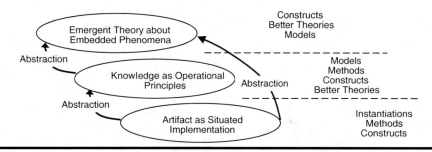

Figure 2.4   Outputs of design science (Purao, 2002).

Explicitly the upper level of Figure 2.4 and implicitly the middle level, knowledge about operational principles, are theories about the emergent properties of the inner environment of the artifact (Simon, 1996). However, in any complex artifact, at either level of abstraction, multiple principles can be invoked simultaneously to explain aspects of the artifact's behavior. In this sense, the behavior of the artifact in any single design science research project is *overdetermined* (Carroll and Kellogg, 1989). This inevitable aspect of design science research has consequences discussed further in the section on "Philosophical Grounding of Design Science Research."

An Example of Community-Determined Outputs

Precisely what is obtained from a design science research effort is determined by (1) the phase of research on which reflection and analysis focuses (from Figure 2.3) and (2) the level of abstraction to which the reflection and analysis generalize (from Figure 2.4). These factors, in turn, are strongly influenced by the community performing the research.

To illustrate the different outputs that are commonly seen as the desired result for design science research, consider the *same* artifact development as carried out by different ICT research sub-communities: database, software engineering, HCI, decision sciences, and IS cognitive researchers (IS Cognitive Research Exchange — IS CORE): the construction of a data visualization interface for complex queries against large relational databases. For all of the communities, the research is motivated by common *problem awareness:* that a better interface can be developed that will allow users to more quickly and effectively obtain answers to questions about the performance of their business operations.

The theoretical impetus for the prospective improvement would vary between research communities. For the software engineering or database communities, the motivation could be new knowledge of faster access techniques or visual rendering techniques. For the decision sciences community and the HCI and cognitive research communities, the impetus could be new research in reference disciplines on visual impacts, on cognition, and on decision making. The resulting artifact would be quite similar for all communities, as would the construction mechanics

How to make better decisions (versus) invest in better processes

Table 2.2 Design Science Research Perspectives and Outputs by Community

Community	Perspective	Knowledge Derived
HCI; IS CORE; decision science	Artifact as experimental apparatus	What database visualization interfaces reveal about the cognition of complex data relationships
Database; decision science software engineering	Artifact as focused design principle exploration	Principles for the construction of data visualization interfaces
Database; software engineering	Artifact as improved instance of tool	A better data visualization interface for relational, business-oriented databases

— the computer languages used in development, the deployment platforms, etc. However, the stages of development on which observation and reflection centered and the measures used to evaluate the resultant artifact (cf. Figure 2.3) would be considerably different for each community. Table 2.2 lists the communities that might construct a data visualization artifact, the primary perspective with which they would view the artifact, and the different knowledge that would emerge from the research effort as a result of the differing perspectives.

Some explications of design science research in IS have stated that the primary focus is always on the finished artifact and how well it works rather than its component interactions, that is, *why* it works (Hevner et al., 2004). Other writers and our example present a broader view. The apparent contradiction may simply be in how wide the net of *IS research* is cast and the selection of sub-communities it is considered to contain.

The Philosophical Grounding of Design Science Research

Ontology is the study that describes the nature of reality. For example, what is real and what is not, what is fundamental and what is derivative?

Epistemology is the study that explores the nature of knowledge. For example, on what does knowledge depend, and how can we be certain of what we know?

Axiology is the study of values. What values does an individual or group hold, and why? *TRUTH* *BELIEFS*

The definitions of these terms are worth reviewing because although assumptions about reality, knowledge, and value underlie any intellectual endeavor, they are *implicit* most of the time for most people, including researchers. Indeed, as historians and philosophers of science have noted, in "tightly" paradigmatic communities, people may conduct research for an entire career without considering the philosophical implications of their passively received areas of interest and research methods

Gure

Table 2.3   Philosophical Assumptions of Three Research Perspectives)

Research Perspective			
Basic Belief	*Positivist*	*Interpretive*	*Design*
Ontology TRUTH	A single reality Knowable, probabilistic	Multiple realities, socially constructed	Multiple, contextually situated alternative world-states Socio-technologically enabled
Epistemology Knowledge	Objective; dispassionate Detached observer of truth	Subjective (i.e., values and knowledge emerge from the researcher-participant interaction)	Knowing through making: objectively constrained construction within a context Iterative circumscription reveals meaning
Methodology	Observation; quantitative, statistical	Participation; qualitative. Hermeneutical, dialectical	Developmental Measure artifactual impacts on the composite system
Axiology: what is of value BELIEFS	Truth: universal and beautiful; prediction	Understanding: situated and description	Control; creation; progress (i.e., improvement); understanding

(Kuhn, 1996; first published in 1962). It is typically only in multi-paradigmatic or pre-paradigmatic communities — such as IS — that researchers are forced to consider the most fundamental bases of the socially constructed realities (Berger and Luckman, 1966; Searle, 1995) in which they operate.

The contrasting ontological and epistemological assumptions implicit in natural science and social science research approaches have been authoritatively explicated in a number of widely cited works (Bunge, 1984; Guba and Lincoln, 1994). Gregg et al. (2001) add the meta-level assumptions of design science research (which they term the "socio-technologist/developmentalist approach") to earlier work contrasting/positivist and interpretive/approaches to research. We have drawn from Gregg et al. in compiling Table 2.3, which summarizes the philosophical assumptions of those three "ways of knowing," and have added several insights from our combined 40+ years of design science research experience. Our first addition is the stress on *iterative circumscription* (cf. Figure 2.3) and how this essential part of the design science research methodology iteratively determines (or reveals) the reality and the knowledge that emerge from the research effort. The second addition to Table 2.3 is the row labeled "Axiology" — the study of values. We believe it is the shared valuing of what researchers hope to find in the pursuit of their efforts that binds them into a community. Certainly the self and community valuation of their efforts and findings is a highly significant motivator for any researcher, and we were surprised to find how little stress this topic has received in the literature, especially given the significant differences in what each community values.

The metaphysical assumptions of design science research are unique. First, neither the ontology, the epistemology, nor the axiology of the paradigm is derivable from any other. Second, ontological and epistemological viewpoints shift in design science research as the project runs through circumscription cycles depicted in Figure 2.3. This iteration is similar to but more radical than the hermeneutic processes used in some interpretive research.

Design science research, by definition, changes the state-of-the-world through the introduction of novel artifacts. Thus, design science researchers are comfortable with alternative world-states. The obvious contrast is with positivist ontology where a single given composite socio-technical system is the typical unit of analysis; even the problem statement is subject to revision as a design science research effort proceeds. However, the multiple world-states of the design science researcher are not the same as the multiple realities of the interpretive researcher: many if not most design science researchers believe in a single, stable underlying physical reality that constrains the multiplicity of world-states. The abductive phase of design science research (Figure 2.3) in which physical laws are tentatively composed into a configuration that will produce an artifact with the intended problem solving functionality virtually demands a natural-science-like belief in a single, fixed grounding reality.

Epistemologically, the design science researcher knows that a piece of information is factual and knows further what that information means through the process of construction and circumscription. An artifact is constructed. Its behavior is the result of interactions between components. Descriptions of the interactions are information and to the degree the artifact behaves predictably the information is true. Its meaning is precisely the functionality it enables in the composite system (artifact and user). What it means is what it does. The design science researcher is thus a pragmatist (Pierce, 1931). There is also a flavor of instrumentalism (Hendry, 2004) in design science research. The dependence on a predictably functioning artifact (instrument) gives design science research an epistemology that resembles that of natural-science research more closely than that of either positivist or interpretive research.

Axiologically, the design science researcher values creative manipulation and control of the environment in addition to (if not over) more traditional research values such as the pursuit of truth or understanding. Certainly the design science researcher must have a far higher tolerance for ambiguity than is generally acceptable in the positivist research stance. As many authors have pointed out, the end result of a design science research effort may be very poorly understood and still be considered a success by the community (Hevner et al., 2004). A practical or functional addition to an area body of knowledge, codified and transmitted to the community where it can provide the basis for further exploration, may be all that is required of a successful project. Indeed, it is precisely in the exploration of "wicked problems" for which conflicting or sparse theoretical bases exist that design science research excels (March and Smith, 1995; Carroll and Kellogg, 1989).

Finally, the philosophical perspective of the design science researcher changes as progress is iteratively made through the phases of Figure 2.3. In some sense, it is as if the design science researcher creates a reality through constructive intervention, then reflectively becomes a positivist observer, recording the behavior of the system and comparing it to the predictions (theory) set out during the abductive phase. The observations are interpreted, become the basis for new theorizing, and a new abductive, interventionist cycle begins. In this sense, design science research is very similar to the action research methodology of the interpretive paradigm; however, the time frame of design science research construction is enormously foreshortened relative to the social group interactions typical of action research.

Bunge (1984) implies that design science research is most effective when its practitioners shift between pragmatic and critical realist perspectives, guided by a pragmatic assessment of progress in the design cycle. Purao (2002) presents a very rich elaboration on the perspective shifts that accompany any iterative design cycle. His analysis is grounded in semiotics and describes in detail how "the design researcher arrives at an interpretation (understanding) of the phenomenon and the design of the artifact simultaneously."

Design Science Research Methodology (By Example)

In this section the general method underlying design science research in its multiplicity of as-practiced variants is described, followed by a discussion of the method as used in a published example of ICT design science research.

The astute reader will recognize Figure 2.5, The general methodology for all design science research, as a variant of Figure 2.3, Reasoning in the general design cycle. This is a logical and inevitable result of the fact that in design science research, *knowing* (Figure 2.3) *is making* (Figure 2.5). To better focus on the process as a research *method*, a column labeled "Outputs" has been substituted for the "Logical Formalism" column.

With reference to Figure 2.5,* a typical design science research effort proceeds as follows:

Awareness of Problem. An awareness of an interesting problem can come from multiple sources: new developments in industry or in a reference discipline. Reading

---

* Note: There are many excellent descriptions (and diagrams) of the process of design science research in IS (cf. Hevner et al., 2004; Purao, 2002; Gregg et al., 2001; March and Smith, 1995; Nunamaker et al., 1991). We chose this diagram because it emphasizes the knowledge generation inherent in the method and because it originated in an analysis of the processes inherent in *any* design effort.

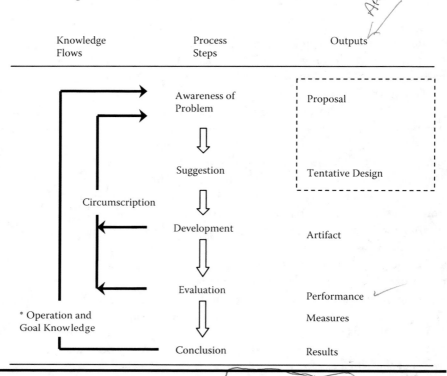

Knowledge Flows	Process Steps	Outputs

Figure 2.5   The general methodology of design science research.

in an allied discipline may also provide the opportunity for application of new findings to the researcher's field. The output of this phase is a Proposal, formal or informal, for a new research effort.

Suggestion. The Suggestion phase follows immediately behind the Proposal and is intimately connected with it, as the dotted line around Proposal and Tentative Design (the output of the Suggestion phase) indicates. Indeed, in any formal proposal for design science research, such as one to be made to the NSF (National Science Foundation) or an industry sponsor, a Tentative Design and likely the performance of a prototype based on that design would be an integral part of the Proposal. Moreover, if after consideration of an interesting problem, a Tentative Design does not present itself to the researcher, the idea (Proposal) will be set aside. Suggestion is an essentially creative step wherein new functionality is envisioned based on a novel configuration of either existing or new and existing elements. The step has been criticized as introducing nonrepeatability into the design science research method; human creativity is still a poorly understood cognitive process. However, the step has necessary analogues in all research methods; for example, in positivist research, creativity is inherent in the leap from curiosity about organizational phenomena to the development of appropriate constructs that operationalize the phenomena and an appropriate research design for their measurement.

Development. The Tentative Design is further developed and implemented in this phase. Elaboration of the Tentative Design into complete design requires creative effort. The techniques for implementation will of course vary, depending on the artifact to be constructed. An algorithm may require construction of a formal proof. An expert system embodying novel assumptions about human cognition in an area of interest will require software development, probably using a high-level package or tool. The implementation itself can be very pedestrian and need not involve novelty beyond the state-of-practice for the given artifact; the novelty is primarily in the design, not the construction of the artifact.

Evaluation. Once constructed, the artifact is evaluated according to criteria that are always implicit and frequently made explicit in the Proposal (Awareness of Problem phase). Deviations from expectations, both quantitative and qualitative, are carefully noted and *must be tentatively explained*. That is, the evaluation phase contains an analytic sub-phase in which hypotheses are made about the behavior of the artifact. This phase exposes an epistemic fluidity that is in stark contrast to a strict interpretation of the positivist stance. At an equivalent point in positivist research, analysis either confirms or contradicts a hypothesis. Essentially, save for some consideration of future work as may be indicated by experimental results, the research effort is finished. For the design science researcher, by contrast, things are just getting interesting. Rarely, in design science research, are initial hypotheses concerning behavior completely borne out. Instead, the evaluation phase results and additional information gained in the construction and running of the artifact are brought together and fed back to another round of Suggestion (cf. the circumscription arrows of Figures 2.3 and 2.5). The explanatory hypotheses, which are quite broad, are rarely discarded; rather, they are modified to be in accord with the new observations. This suggests a new design, frequently preceded by new library research in directions suggested by deviations from theoretical performance. (Design science researchers seem to share Allen Newell's concept [from cognitive science] of theories as complex, robust nomological networks.) This concept has been observed by philosophers of science in many communities (Lakatos, 1978); and working from it, Newell suggests that theories are not like clay pigeons, to be blasted to bits with the Popperian shotgun of falsification. Rather, they should be treated like doctoral students. One corrects them when they err, and is hopeful they can amend their flawed behavior and go on to be evermore useful and productive (Newell, 1990).

Conclusion. This phase is the finale of a specific research effort. Typically, it is the result of satisficing; that is, although there are still deviations in the behavior of the artifact from the (multiply) revised hypothetical predictions, the results are adjudged "good enough." Not only are the results of the effort consolidated and "written up" at this phase, but the knowledge gained in the effort is frequently categorized as either "firm" — facts that have been learned and can be repeatedly applied or behavior that can be repeatedly invoked — or as "loose ends" — anomalous behavior that defies explanation and may well serve as the subject of further research.

An Example of ICT Design Science Research

The example chosen here to add detail and concreteness to the discussion of design science research philosophy and method in ICT is one from the joint experience of the authors. We make only two claims for this research: (1) it is a reasonable example because it comfortably encompasses all the points of the preceding discussion; and (2) because it is our research, we are privy to and able to present a multitude of details that are rarely written up and available in journal publications. We describe the research, from conception to the first publication to be drawn from it, in phases corresponding to those in Figures 2.3 and 2.5.

Smart Object Paradigm: A Design Science Research Project

Awareness of Problem

In the mid-1980s, one of the senior project participants, Vaishnavi, began actively seeking to extend his research from designing efficient data and file structures (a primarily computer science topic) to software engineering (an area with a significant IS component). In the course of a discussion with one of his colleagues at Georgia State University (GSU), he became aware of a situation that showed research promise: the development of a computerized decision support system for nuclear reactors. Three Mile Island had brought national awareness to the problems associated with the safe operation of a nuclear power plant, rule-based decision support systems were a current area of general IS interest, and the director of the research reactor at Georgia Tech was interested in developing a system to support its operations.

A doctoral student (Gary Buchanan) was brought into the project to begin a preliminary support system development in the rule-based language Prolog. Within a few weeks it became apparent that a system to support the several thousand procedures found in a typical commercial power plant would be nearly impossible to develop in Prolog; and if developed, it would be literally impossible to maintain. The higher-level expert system development packages available at the time (and currently) were more capable but still obviously inadequate. The difficulty in constructing and maintaining large expert systems was widely known at the time; however, the Prolog pilot project gave the research group significant insight they would not otherwise have had into the root causes of the problem: continuously changing requirements and the complexity inherent in several thousand rule-based interlocking procedures. Out of a detailed analysis of the failed pilot system emerged the first *awareness of the problem* on which the research would focus: how to construct and continuously maintain a support system for the operation of a complex, hierarchical, procedure-driven environment.

Suggestion

There are many approaches to the problems of software system complexity, and the research group discussed them over a period of months. Some of the alternatives that were discarded included development of a new software development methodology specifically focused on operation support systems, automation of the maintenance function, and development of a high-level programming environment. New insights into the problem continued to emerge even as (and precisely because) potential solutions to the problem were considered. One key insight was that the system complexity resided primarily in control of the system; that is, although the individual procedures could be modeled in a straightforward manner, the procedure that should take precedence (control) over the others and where the results of that procedure should be routed depended in a highly complex fashion on past and present states of multiple procedures. Essential to the development of the system was the effective modeling of this complex control structure.

By this point, Buchanan had decided to adopt the problem as his dissertation topic and under Vijay Vaishnavi's direction began extensive research into various mechanisms for modeling (describing in a precise, formal way) control. As the realization grew that they were in effect seeking to describe the *semantics* of the system, his reading began to focus especially on some of the techniques to emerge from the area of semantic modeling.

During the alternating cycles of discussion, reading, and individual cogitation that characterize many design science research efforts, several software engineering concepts were brought together with a final key insight to yield the ultimately successful direction for the development. During one discussion, Vaishnavi realized that the control information for the system was *knowledge*, identical in form to the domain knowledge in the procedures and could be modeled with rules, in the same way. However, because the execution of the individual procedures was independent of the control knowledge, the two types of rules could execute in different cycles, partitioning and greatly reducing the complexity of the overall system. Finally, the then relatively new concept of object orientation seemed the ideal approach to partitioning the total system knowledge into individual procedures. And if each "smart" object were further partitioned into a domain knowledge and an control knowledge component, and if the rules were stated in a high-level English-like syntax that was both executable and readable by domain experts...

Awareness of Problem Revisited

As noted in the general discussion of the design science research method, any of its phases can be spontaneously revisited from any of the other phases. Especially in the early stages of a project, this results in a conceptual fluidity that can be disconcerting to practitioners of less dynamic paradigms. Although it is difficult in retrospect to pinpoint exactly where in the process the change occurred, by the inception of the development phase, the problem statement had changed to a sub-goal implicit in the original problem statement: *how to effectively model operations support systems for complex, hierarchical, procedure driven environments.* (This sort of "drilling-down" into the problem or re-scoping the research at a more basic level occurs frequently in all research, but is effectively part of the method in design science research.)

Development

Although the development of a design science research artifact can be straightforward, that was not the case for the smart object paradigm. The construction was completely conceptual and involved the "discovery" through multiple thought and paper trials of the details of the central novel entity that had been conceptualized at a high level in the Suggestion phase, the "smart object."

For example, what (exactly) would the syntax be for the two types of rules, domain and control? How (exactly) should the two rule evaluation cycles for each type of knowledge interleave? Should the two types of knowledge be permitted to interact? If so, how? Should control rules have the ability to "write" or "rescind" domain rules, a la Lisp? Or vice versa?

In a conceptual development such as this, the suggestion and construction phases blur because a successful design decision *is* an output product. The final deliverable (from this initial development) was a conceptual model consisting of (1) a set of meta-level rules for implementing domain knowledge and control knowledge separately, but within a single structure, the "smart object"; and (2) another set of meta-rules that described how the domain and control knowledge, once "modeled" as smart objects, would be interpreted (a virtual machine for executing the smart objects).

Evaluation

In a sense, evaluation takes place continuously in a design process (research or otherwise) because a large number of "micro-evaluations" take place at every design detail decision. Each decision is followed by a "thought experiment" in which that part of the design is mentally exercised by the designer. However, for the remainder of this section we describe the "formal" evaluation that occurred after the design had stabilized.

To test the conceptual design, various operating environments were modeled and "hand-stepped" through the execution rules to determine that logically correct system behavior occurred at appropriate times in the simulation. The simulation that appeared in Buchanan's dissertation (1991), the first publication to result from the research, was a grocery-bagging "robot." This example had been popularized in a best-selling artificial intelligence textbook of the time and had the advantage of being a familiar logic test bed to many external evaluators of the artifact. Exponents of other research paradigms may find the evaluation criteria simplistic, and wonder why, for example, modeling of the nuclear power plant operating environment was not the obvious choice. The answer is: resources; the modeling and hand testing of even the grocery-bagging example occupied several man-months. During the evaluation, minor redesign of the artifact (the smart object conceptual model) occurred on several occasions, which is a common occurrence in design science research. By the end of the evaluation phase, the smart object model had successfully completed simulation of numerous bagging exercises and was adjudged a success by the design team.

Conclusion

The finale for the first research effort involving smart objects was the codification of the problem development, design basis in prior work, the design itself, and the results of the evaluation effort in Buchanan's dissertation (1991). The successful defense of the dissertation at Georgia State required careful consideration and judgment of the artifact and its performance by a committee composed primarily of other design science researchers. The core concepts were considered to have substantial merit, and Buchanan and Vaishnavi produced several conference papers based on smart objects.

Epilogue

After Buchanan's graduation, both he and Vaishnavi collaborated on a paper based on the research project and submitted it to *IEEE Transactions on Data and Knowledge Engineering* (*TDKE*). The paper was returned for substantial revisions. At this point, Buchanan's interest in the project waned; however, a recently admitted GSU CIS doctoral student (Bill Kuechler) found the concepts interesting enough to enter into the research group and continue the development effort. After four years, four conference papers on smart objects and related topics, and three major revisions, the *TDKE* paper was finally published as "A Data/Knowledge Paradigm for the Modeling and Design of Operations Support Systems" (Vaishnavi et al., 1997). By the time of acceptance, smart objects had been through several additional design science research cycles, each focusing on the refinement of a different aspect of the original design, or a critical support function for its use-in-practice such as the methodology developed for partitioning workflow information into smart objects.

Design Science Research versus Design

A significant and valid question posed frequently to design science researchers is: how is your research different from a design effort; what makes your work research and not simply state-of-practice design?

We propose that design science research is distinguishable from design by the *production of interesting (to a community) new knowledge.* In a typical *industry* design effort, a new product (artifact) is produced; but in most cases, the more successful the project is considered to be, the less is learned. That is, it is generally desirable to produce a new product using state-of-practice application of state-of-practice techniques and readily available components. In fact, most product design efforts in industry are preceded by many meetings designed to "engineer the risk out of" the design effort. The risks that are identified in such meetings are the "we don't know how to do this yet" areas that are precisely the targets of design science research efforts. This is in no way meant to diminish the creativity that is essential to any design effort. We merely wish to point out that design is readily distinguishable from design science research (within its community of interest) by the intellectual risk, the number of unknowns in the proposed design, which when successfully surmounted provide the new information that makes the effort research and assures its value.

References and Bibliography

General References on Design Science Research

Alexander, C. (1964). *Notes on the Synthesis of Form*. Cambridge, MA: Harvard University Press.

Carroll, J. and Kellogg, W. (1989). Artifact as Theory Nexus: Hermeneutics Meets Theory-Based Design. In *Proceedings of CHI '89*, ACM Press.

Dasgupta, S. (1996). *Technology and Creativity*. New York: Oxford University Press.

Gregg, D., Kulkarni, U., et al. (2001). Understanding the Philosophical Underpinnings of Software Engineering Research in Information Systems. *Information Systems Frontiers*, 3(2), 169–183.

Hevner, A., March, S., Park, J., and Ram, S. (2004). Design Science in Information Systems Research. *MIS Quarterly*, 28(1), 75–105.

Kuhn, T. (1996). *The Structure of Scientific Revolutions*. Chicago: University of Chicago Press.

Lakatos, I. (1978). *The Methodology of Scientific Research Programmes*. Worral, J. and Currie, G., Eds. Cambridge: Cambridge University Press.

March, S. and Smith, G. (1995). Design and Natural Science Research on Information Technology. *Decision Support Systems,* 15, 251–266.

Maturana, H. and Varela, F. (1987). *The Tree of Knowledge: The Biological Roots of Human Understanding.* Boston, MA: New Science Library.

McCarthy, J. (1980). Circumscription —A Form of Non-Monotonic Reasoning. *Artificial Intelligence*, 13, 27–39. ON LINE STANFORD VERSION 1988

Owen, C. (1997). Design Research: Building the Knowledge Base. *Journal of the Japanese Society for the Science of Design,* 5(2), 36–45.

Orlikowski, W. and C. Iacono (2001). Desperately Seeking the "IT" in IT Research — A Call to Theorizing the IT Artifact. *Information Systems Research*, 12(2), 121–134.

Pierce, C. S: Collected Papers. Harshorne, C. and Weiss, P., Eds. Cambridge, MA: Harvard University Press, (1931–1935).

Purao, S. (2002). Design Research in the Technology of Information Systems: Truth or Dare. GSU Department of CIS Working Paper. Atlanta, GA.

Rossi, M. and Sein, M. (2003). Design Research Workshop: A Proactive Research Approach. Presentation delivered at *IRIS 26*, August 9–12, 2003. http://tiesrv.hkkk.fi/iris26/presentation/workshop_designRes.pdf, last accessed January 16, 2004.

Simon, H. (1996). *The Sciences of the Artificial*, third edition. Cambridge, MA: MIT Press.

Takeda, H., Veerkamp, P., Tomiyama, T., and Yoshikawam, H. (1990). Modeling Design Processes. *AI Magazine*, Winter, 37–48.

Varela, F. (1988). Structural Coupling and the Origin of Meaning in a Simple Cellular Automata. In *The Semiotics of Cellular Communication in the Immune System*. Scaraz, E., Celada, F., Michenson, N., and Tada, T., Eds. New York: Springer-Verlag.

Walls, J., Widmeyer, G., and El Sawy, O. (1992). Building an Information System Design Theory for Vigilant EIS. *Information Systems Research*, 3(1), 36–59.

References on Philosophical Grounding of Design Science Research

Ackoff, R. (1962). The nature of science and methodology. In *Scientific Method: Optimizing Applied Research Decisions*, Ackoff, R., Ed. New York: John Wiley & Sons, chap. 2.

Berger, P. and Luckman, T. (1966). *The Social Construction of Reality: A Treatise in the Sociology of Knowledge.* Garden City, New York: Doubleday.

Bunge, M. (1984). Philosophical Inputs and Outputs of Technology. *History and Philosophy of Technology*. Bugliarello, G. and Donner, D., Eds. Urbana, IL: University of Illinois Press, pp. 263–281.

Carroll, J. and Kellogg, W. (1989). Artifact as Theory Nexus: Hermeneutics Meets Theory-Based Design. In *Proceedings of CHI '89*, ACM Press.

Dasgupta, S. (1996). *Technology and Creativity*. New York: Oxford University Press.

Gregg, D., Kulkarni, U., and Vinze, A. (2001). Understanding the Philosophical Underpinnings of Software Engineering Research in Information Systems. *Information Systems Frontiers,* 3(2), 169–183.

Guba, E. and Lincoln, Y. (1994). Competing Paradigms in Qualitative Research. *The Handbook of Qualitative Research.* Denzin, N. and Lincoln, Y., Eds. Thousand Oaks, CA: Sage, pp. 105–117.

Hendry, R. (2004). Are Realism and Instrumentalism Methodologically Different? Online working paper, Department of Philosophy, University of Durham, U.K., last accessed January 11, 2004. URL: http://hypatia.ss.uci.edu/lps/psa2k/realism-and-instrumentalism. pdf Author e-mail: r.f.hendry@dur.ac.uk

Hevner, A., March, S., Park, J., and Ram, S. (2004). Design Science in Information Systems Research. *MIS Quarterly*, 28(1), 75–105.

Kuhn, T. (1996). *The Structure of Scientific Revolutions*. Chicago: University of Chicago Press.

March, S. and Smith, G. (1995). Design and Natural Science Research on Information Technology. *Decision Support Systems*, 15, 251–266.

Pierce, C.S: Collected Papers. Harshorne, C. and P. Weiss, Eds. Cambridge, MA: Harvard University Press, (1931–1935).

Purao, S. (2002). Design Research in the Technology of Information Systems: Truth or Dare. GSU Department of CIS Working Paper. Atlanta, GA.

Saraswat, P. (2004). A Historical Perspective on the Philosophical Foundations of Information Systems. Document online at the Web site of <AIS SIGPhilosophy, AIS> at: http://www.bauer.uh.edu/parks/fis/saraswat3.htm.

Searle, J., Ed. (1995). *The Construction of Social Reality*. New York: The Free Press.

References on Design Science Research Methodology

Buchanan, G. (1991). Modeling Operations Management Support Systems. Unpublished doctoral dissertation, Atlanta, GA. College of Business Administration, Georgia State University.

Gregg, D., Kulkarni, U., and Vinze, A. (2001). Understanding the Philosophical Underpinnings of Software Engineering Research in Information Systems. *Information Systems Frontiers*, 3(2), 169–183.

Hevner, A., March, S., Park, J., and Ram, S. (2004). Design Science in Information Systems Research. *MIS Quarterly*, 28(1), 75–105.

Lakatos, I. (1978) *The Methodology of Scientific Research Programmes*, Worral, J. and Currie, G., Eds. Cambridge: Cambridge University Press.

March, S. and Smith, G. (1995). Design and Natural Science Research on Information Technology. *Decision Support Systems*, 15, 251–266.

Newell, A. (1990). *Unified Theories of Cognition*. Cambridge, MA: Harvard University Press.

Nunamaker, J., Chen, M., and Purdin, T. (1991). System Development in Information Systems Research. *Journal of Management Information Systems*, 7(3), 89–106.

Purao, S. (2002). Design Research in the Technology of Information Systems: Truth or Dare. GSU Department of CIS Working Paper. Atlanta, GA.

Shu, N. (1988). Axiomatic Design Theory for Systems. *Research in Engineering Design*, 10, 189–209.

Vaishnavi, V., Buchanan, G., and Kuechler, W. (1997). A Data/Knowledge Paradigm for the Modeling and Design of Operations Support Systems, *IEEE Transactions on Knowledge and Data Engineering*, 9(2), 275–291.

Zelkowitz, M. and Wallace, D. (1998). "Experimental Models for Validating Technology." IEEE Computer, 31(5), 23–31.

References on Understanding Design Science Research in the Context of Information Systems Research

Adams, L. and Courtney, J. (2004). Achieving Relevance in IS Research via the DAGS Framework. *Proc. of the 37th Hawaii International Conference on System Sciences.*

Alter, S. (2003). 18 Reasons Why IT-Reliant Work Systems Should Replace "The IT Artifact" as the Core Subject Matter of the IS Field. *Communications of the AIS*, 12, 365–394.

Applegate, L. (1999). Rigor and Relevance in MIS Research — Introduction. *MIS Quarterly*, 23(1), 1–2.

Benbasat, I. and Zmud, R. (1999). Empirical Research in Information Systems: The Practice of Relevance. *MIS Quarterly*, 23(1), 3–16.

Brooks, F. (1996). The Computer Scientist as Toolsmith II. *Communications of the ACM*, 39(3), 61–68.

Caws, P. (1969). The Structure of Discovery. *Science*, 166, 1375–1380.

Falconer, D. and Mackay, D. (1999). Ontological Problems of Pluralist Research Methodologies. *5th AIS Conference on Information Systems*, Milwaukee, WI.

Fugetta, A. (1999). Some Reflections on Software Engineering Research. *ACM SIGSOFT Software Engineering Notes,* 24(1), 74–77.

Glass, R. (1999). On Design. *IEEE Software*, 16(2), 103–104.

Glass, R., Ramesh, V., and Vessey, I. (2004). An analysis of research computing disciplines. *Communications of the ACM*, 47(6), 89–84.

Hempel, C. (1966). *Philosophy of Natural Science.* Englewood Cliffs, NJ: Prentice Hall.

Hopcroft, J. (1987). Computer Science: The Emergence of a Discipline. *Communications of the ACM*, 30(3), 198–202.

Iivari, J. (2003). The IS CORE VII: Towards Information Systems as a Science of Meta-Artifacts. *Communication of the AIS,* 12(October), Article 37.

Kleindorfer, G., O'Neill, L., and Ganeshan, R. (1998). Validation in Simulation: Various Positions in the Philosophy of Science. *Management Science*, 44(8), 1087–1099.

Lee, A. (2000). Systems Thinking, Design Science and Paradigms: Heeding Three Lessons from the Past to Resolve Three Dilemmas in the Present to Direct a Trajectory for Future Research in the Information Systems Field. Keynote address at the *11th International Conference on Information Management.* http://www.people.vcu.edu/~aslee/ICIM-keynote-2000 last accessed January, 16, 2004.

March, S., Hevner, A., and Ram, S. (2000). Research Commentary: An Agenda for Information Technology Research in Heterogeneous and Distributed Environments. *Information Systems Research*, 11(4), 327–341.

Morrison, J. and George, J. (1995). Exploring the Software Engineering Component of MIS Research. *Communications of the ACM*, 38(7), 80–91.

Newell, A. and Simon H. (1976). Computer Science as Empirical Inquiry: Symbols and Search. *Communications of the ACM*, 19(3), 113–126.

Norman, D. (1988). *The Design of Everyday Things.* New York: Doubleday.

Parnas, D. (1998). Successful Software Engineering Research. *ACM SIGSOFT Software Engineering Notes,* 23(3), 64-68.

Petroski, H. (1996). *Invention by Design: How Engineers Get from Thought to Thing.* Cambridge, MA: Harvard University Press.

Petter, S., Vaishnavi, V., and Hsieh, J. (2003). Linking Theory with Practice: A Research Approach and Illustration of its Use in Software Project Management. Working Paper, Department of Computer Information Systems, Georgia State University.

Popper, K. (1980). Science: Conjectures and Refutations. *Introductory Readings in the Philosophy of Science*. Hollinger, R. and Kline, A., Eds. New York: Prometheus Books, 29–34.

Robey, D. (1996). Research Commentary: Diversity in Information Systems Research: Threat, Opportunity and Responsibility. *Information Systems Research*, 7(4), 400–408.

Schon, D. (1993). *The Reflective Practitioner: How Professionals Think in Action*. New York: Basic Books.

Tichy, W. (1998). Should Computer Scientists Experiment More? *IEEE Computer*, 31(5), 32–40.

Tsichritzis, D. (1997). The Dynamics of Innovation. Beyond Calculation: The Next Fifty Years of Computing, Denning, P. and Metcaffe, R., Eds. New York: Springer-Verlag, pp. 259–265.

Truex, D. (2001). Three Issues Concerning Relevance in IS Research: Epistemology, Audience and Method. *Communications of the AIS*, 6:24.

Vaishnavi, V. and Kuechler, W. (2004). Design Research in Information Systems, January 20, 2004. URL: http://www.isworld.org/Researchdesign/drisISworld.htm Authors e-mail: vvaishna@gsu.edu kuechler@unr.edu.

Weber, R. (1987). Toward a Theory of Artifacts: A Paradigmatic Base for Information Systems Research. *Journal of Information Systems,* Spring, 3–19.

Winograd, T. (1996). *Bringing Design to Software*. Reading, MA: Addison-Wesley.

Winograd, T. (1997). The Design of Interaction. *Beyond Calculation: The Next Fifty Years of Computing*. Denning, P. and Metcaffe, R., Eds. New York: Springer-Verlag, 149–162.

Chapter 3

The Aggregate General Design Cycle as a Perspective on the Evolution of Computing Communities of Interest*

William Kuechler, Vijay K. Vaishnavi, and Stacie Petter

[*Editorial Preface*: The general design cycle (GDC) (see Figures 2.3 and 3.1), in addition to being an empirically observed description of individual (or project team) design activity across multiple fields, is a powerful framework for understanding intellectual development at broader levels of human activity. This chapter expands on the GDC so that the actors are *communities* — of practice or research — and in each iteration throughout the cycle, different communities, united only by a common interest in some aspect of a broadly useful artifact (for example, databases), pass information between each other via journals and other media, conferences, and social networks. From this perspective, information and communication

---

* Adapted from the authors' article in *Computing Letters*, 1(3), 123–128, 2005.

technology (ICT) design science research projects can be seen not only to use the GDC, but also to participate in a broader, inter-group intellectual conversation modeled by a collective version of the GDC — that is, the A(ggregate)GDC.]

Introduction

Insight into the subject emphasis of a research community is valuable information both for the members of that community and its related areas, and for determining the degree of alignment between the research community and commercial applications of the research (Culnan, 1987). Knowledge of the mechanisms by which a research community chooses to direct its resources is also of interest to the academic community in general, and to researchers in organizational behavior and dynamics, including those interested in group decision theory and concept diffusion through groups (Alavi et al., 1989). Research by several authors supports the commonsense observation that a *research community* is actually an aggregation of "invisible colleges" (Culnan, 1987; Pfeffer et al., 1977), each with specific research directions, under a common "umbrella" heading. The common heading is an accurate gauge of general direction but is always broad enough to support (and require) meaningful sub-topics "which tend to concentrate on examining common [highly specific] questions in common ways" (Pfeffer et al., 1977). Yet despite interest in understanding research directions, no research that we are aware of has attempted to model the dynamics of an extended research community.

In an earlier chapter, we developed a cognitive model of design — the general design cycle (GDC) — into a descriptive model of *design science research*, the *generation of knowledge through making* that typifies information and communication technology (ICT) and many engineering fields (Vaishnavi and Kuechler, 2004). This chapter first explains the GDC framework as a research approach to create an artifact. It then shows how the GDC in aggregate form can be interpreted as a framework for understanding how multiple streams of ICT research from varying disciplines converge to support the evolution of a complex computing artifact over time.

The General Design Cycle

Takeda et al. (1990) have analyzed the reasoning that occurs in the course of a GDC. Vaishnavi and Kuechler (2004) have extended this analysis to explicate the knowledge generated in a design effort and apply the cycle specifically to design science research as illustrated in Figure 3.1. In following the flow of creative effort through this diagram, the types of new knowledge that arise from design activities and the reason that this knowledge is most readily found during a design effort will become apparent.

Design science research is sometimes called "improvement research," and this designation emphasizes the problem-solving and performance-improving nature of the

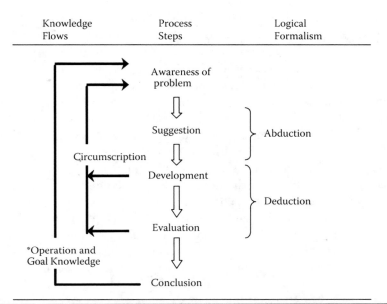

Figure 3.1 **Reasoning in the general design cycle (GDC). (*An operational principle can be defined as "any technique or frame of reference about a class of artifacts or its characteristics that facilitates creation, manipulation, and modification of artifactual forms" (Dasgupta, 2000; Purao, 2002).)**

activity. In this model, all design begins with Awareness of Problem. The problem may be identified by a literature review, an experience in practice, or even conversations with colleagues. In the Awareness of Problem phase, the problem is not only identified, but also defined. Explicit use of the GDC prompts researchers to spend "more time defining the problem before deciding to build a tool" (Purao, 2002). To properly define the problem, an initial literature review should attempt to (1) determine that the problem has not been previously solved and determine what, if any, research has been previously performed in the area; (2) determine that the problem is widespread and that the solution will be an interesting contribution to the practice and academic communities; (3) define and scope the problem as appropriate for the resources available to the project. Gaps in current research should become readily apparent.

Suggestions for a problem solution are abductively drawn from the existing knowledge or theory base for the problem area (Pierce, 1931), or developed using an appropriate research methodology. Existing literature may be a sufficient guide to provide suggestions on the artifact to be developed; however, conducting an explanation research study* can also be helpful in identifying potential suggestions.

---

* While design science research seeks to solve a problem or improve practice, explanation research aims to understand why a phenomenon occurs through the use of quantitative and qualitative research data collection and analysis.

The research conducted at the Suggestion phase is used to create a Tentative Design for the artifact.

An attempt at implementing the artifact according to the suggested solution (or Tentative Design) is performed next. This stage is shown as Development in the diagram. This phase of the GDC framework is where most of the actual design takes place, which is the creative effort required in synthesizing existing knowledge and a well-defined problem into an artifact for solving the problem. This is the only phase of the GDC that requires a constructivist methodology. The artifact developed in this stage may be rather abstract in nature, such as constructs, models, or methods, or can be more tangible in the form of computing software or hardware (March and Smith, 1995). In the Development phase, the artifact's instantiation may be rather rudimentary as one focuses on design, rather than the implementation of the artifact (Vaishnavi and Kuechler, 2004).

Partially or fully successful implementations are then evaluated according to the functional specification implicit or explicit in the suggestion (Evaluation phase). After developing an artifact, it is necessary to evaluate the artifact using empirical methods "to determine how well an artifact works" (Hevner et al., 2004). Researchers should evaluate their artifacts using methods and techniques similar to theory testing (March and Smith, 1995), including action research, controlled experiments, simulation, or scenarios. The evaluation portion of the design science research approach does not signify a conclusion to research, but rather an opportunity to further refine the artifact through insight and suggestion (see the Circumscription arrow in Figure 3.1; Vaishnavi and Kuechler, 2004).

Development, Evaluation, and further Suggestion are frequently iteratively performed in the course of the research (design) effort. The basis of the iteration, the flow from partial completion of the cycle back to Awareness of Problem, is indicated by the Circumscription arrow. Conclusion indicates termination of a specific design project. The development of Figure 3.1 as the cognitive underpinning of design science research (Hevner et al., 2004), applied to information systems (IS), is developed fully in Vaishnavi and Kuechler (2004).

The Aggregate General Design Cycle

The GDC (Figure 3.1), in the context of design science research, shows the design effort in-the-small, that is, as used for an individual design (artifact construction) effort. Even at that level, an analysis of the cycle in use shows that each phase (Awareness of Problem, Suggestion, etc.) comprises a sometimes brief but completely articulated research effort in itself. For example, "An Example of ICT Design Science Research" in Chapter 2 and Vaishnavi and Kuechler (2004) describe a design science research effort longitudinally and, in that example, the Awareness of Problem stage involved several months of field investigation in the area of interest; the Suggestion stage likewise involved extensive library research

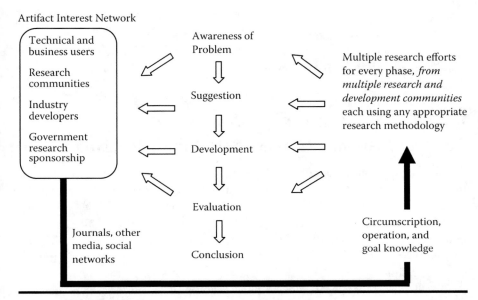

Artifact Interest Network

Figure 3.2 Aggregate general design cycle (AGDC).

and a pilot development program; and so on through all the phases. Although the ultimate intent of the process as a whole was the production of an artifact to support a specific type of development effort, each stage of the cycle was a distinct research effort involving a methodology appropriate to gathering the information required at that stage of development. Frequently, the research phases did not use a constructivist methodology, but rather a meta-bibliographic study or survey, a structured interview in a field setting, a small action research effort, or ethnography.

We propose that an aggregated form of the GDC, which we term the "aggregate general design cycle" (AGDC), is an accurate depiction of a collective, longitudinal research stream in many areas of ICT research. The AGDC shown in Figure 3.2 is an abstraction of the GDC and includes (1) the aggregation of research and development efforts from multiple research programs in multiple communities into an *interest network* for the artifact and (2) the dissemination of knowledge and insights from the network back to individual research efforts. By collective research stream, we mean the accumulated efforts of many researchers who are considered to have a common focus. The focus can nearly always be taken as the artifact produced by the development phase. The *artifact interest network* provides the only coordination available or needed to make a coherent stream from otherwise disjointed efforts contributed by different individuals or groups in different places at different times. The Development phase of the AGDC will use a constructivist methodology to create or enhance an artifact. Just as the GDC uses different information-gathering techniques in each of its phases, research efforts in any of the other phases of the AGDC will use any methodology appropriate for gathering the information required to motivate or evaluate the artifact. Indeed, the researchers involved in the other phases of an aggregate research stream (considered through the lens of the AGDC) may be surprised to see themselves as part of what we consider in our framework as an extended development effort.

Exercising the AGDC Framework: Concept Mapping 25 Years of Database Research

We confine our empirical support for the AGDC as an explanatory framework to one area: database research. We have drawn from an earlier work in which we concept-mapped (Eden, 1992) more than 500 papers from multiple communities on database research, use, and development written over a 25-year period (Kuechler and Beranek, 1994, 2005); however, we believe the same technique applied to any significant ICT artifact (e.g., the World Wide Web) would provide similar findings.

The first "database" papers were purely conceptual, focusing on the obvious desirability (Awareness of Problem, from Figure 3.2) of having a data store detached from computer programs themselves. The vision of an integrated computer-accessible data store that would permit queries to support decision making actually predates the use of computers in business (Bush, 1945). More conceptual papers followed (Suggestion), and prototypes of early databases were developed both in academic and industry settings (Development) (Bachman, 1972). The military has always been influential in database research, primarily through research grants and early adoption of technologies. The earliest versions of the COBOL language contained advanced (for the time) information retrieval and manipulation commands largely due to the military influence.

Once databases began to be used in business, the *artifact network of interest* expanded from the computer science community and the development labs of large corporations to include business and the nascent management information systems (MIS) community, at that time housed in the management science colleges of larger universities. Papers concerned with technical and business use of databases and their implementation in business settings began to appear; they examined the usefulness and impact of databases in business (Evaluation). The Evaluation phase exposed a new set of problems inherent in isolated data structures (feedback from the artifact interest network to research programs; the heavy black line in Figure 3.2), and a new round of conceptual papers began (Awareness of Problem, and Suggestion). A widely cited paper that influenced database use in business and indirectly set research agendas for computer science and information systems researchers for many years was Richard Nolan's 1973 *Harvard Business Review* paper entitled "Computer Data Bases: The Future Is Now" (Nolan, 1973). At a time when IS was still termed "EDP" (electronic data processing), Nolan's critique of information "silos" and call for organization-wide databases set out requirements for the database artifact that would take decades of technological research and development to realize.

Our meta-bibliographic study of the database area shows the same progression through the AGDC phases in cycles for each of the major technical advances in databases: hierarchical, relational, object oriented (multimedia). Moreover, as the importance (synonymous with *general use*) of the artifact increased, more communities became involved in the artifact network of interest. For example, the accounting community, over many years, has produced Evaluation phase research on the difficulties of audit and control (security) of databases, a topic that has led to major streams of research in the ICT fields. As early as 1971, papers appeared in social science journals that foresaw the impact of databases on organizational work habits and on privacy issues (Awareness of Problem, Suggestion, and Evaluation phases in Figure 3.2) (Trystam, 1971). The impact of these papers on technical research was indirect, providing the background that underlay continuous support for research in database security, transaction processing, and backup.

Using the AGDC to Explain Coordination between Diverse Groups

A primary contribution of the AGDC model is to expose the frequently invisible interaction and support that normally disparate communities provide to each other through the artifact interest network. The interactions are complex and, between communities, indirect, which contributes to their invisibility. Various research groups are highly focused on frequently divergent goals that make direct communication between groups unlikely. For example, MIS academics have an organizational rather than a technical focus, and may publish research in management journals that is broadly influential on an artifact yet will never be read by the technical researchers or developers whose artifacts are changed as a result. More concretely, in 20 years in industry, the first author (of this chapter) does not recall reading a single accounting or MIS paper on the implementation of computing artifacts. However, the business people with whom he consulted drew their ideas on database implementation exclusively from these media. They communicated their (frequently inscrutable) requirements to him, and he communicated these in turn to the industry developers of the products he sold and installed.

Conclusion

The authors believe that the AGDC model reflects a sociological reality — it describes how computing research and development for a complex artifact actually originates and evolves over time. If one considers each community in the AGDC as a node in a nomological network, it is readily apparent that the centroid of that network is the artifact produced by the Development phase of the AGDC.

More generally, one can view the history of computing and information systems as a loosely coupled nomological network of AGDCs, each centered on a specific computing-related artifact. Within each AGDC, one can observe the process to have occurred as follows:

- A problem reaches a level of critical interest within the research community and an artifact is produced.
- The artifact is then investigated by researchers with differing backgrounds, interests, goals, and research traditions, all seeking to understand some aspect of this new phenomenon.
- When a sufficient body of research has accumulated, we propose that the accumulated research centered on this new artifact invariably, although without conscious coordination, takes the form we have described as an AGDC.
- If the artifact is sufficiently interesting or commercially or culturally significant, research in all phases of its AGDC continues, operating as a self-organizing complex system with the artifact as its primary attractor (Mikhailov and Calenbuhr, 2002).

We have shown, through a meta-bibliographic study of the database literature over 25 years, that the AGDC model applies to this artifact, and proposed that a similar analysis of any computing artifact will demonstrate the interaction between communities described by the AGDC as its evolution is traced. The model is currently incomplete; the actual dynamics of inter-group communication lie within the artifact interest network, a black box in our model. Various aspects of the diffusion of information within and across groups have been explored by sociologists, IS and other organizational researchers (Alavi et al., 1989), and philosophers of science (Kuhn, 1996). However, other significant artifact coordination mechanisms have never been studied; large corporations such as IBM and NCR have always served as information clearinghouses for business, industry, and academic research, yet we did not find any studies on the mechanism or effect of this important coordination nexus. Incorporating new work in these areas and prior findings into the AGDC model is an interesting area for future research.

References

Alavi, M., Carlson, P., and Brooke, G. (1989). The Ecology of MIS Research: A Twenty Year Review. *Proceedings of the 10th International Conference on Information Systems*, pp. 363–375.

Bachman, C. (1972). The Evolution of Storage Structures. Communications of the ACM, 15(7), 628–634.

Bush, V. (1945). As We May Think. *Atlantic Monthly*, 176(1), 101–108.

Culnan, M. (1987). Mapping the Intellectual Structure of MIS: 1980–1985: A Co-Citation Analysis. MIS Quarterly, 11(3), 341–353.

Dasgupta, S. (1996). Technology and Creativity. New York: Oxford University Press.

Eden, C. (1992). On the Nature of Cognitive Maps. Journal of Management Studies, 29(3), 261–265.

Hevner, A., March, S., Park, J., and Ram, S. (2004). Design Science in Information Systems Research. MIS Quarterly, 28(1), 75–105.

Kuechler, W. and Beranek, M. (2005; 1994). The Intellectual Structure of Database Research: Meta View of a Research Community. Proceedings of Georgia Research on Information Technology and Systems, 1994 (updated and revised for journal submission 06/2005, http://www.unr.edu/homepage/kuechler/meta.html).

Kuhn, T. (1996). The Structure of Scientific Revolutions, third edition. Chicago: The University of Chicago Press.

March, S. and Smith, G. (1995). Design and Natural Science Research on Information Technology. Decision Support Systems, 15(4), 251–266.

Mikhailov, A. and Calenbuhr, V. (2002). From Cells to Societies: Models of Complex Coherent Action. New York: Springer.

Nolan, R. (1973). Computer Data Bases: The Future is Now. Harvard Business Review, 6(2), 98–114.

Pfeffer, J., Leong, A., and Strehl, K. (1977). Paradigm Development and Particularism: Journal Publication in Three Scientific Disciplines. Social Forces, 55(4), 938–951.

Pierce, C.S. (1931). Collected Papers, Harshorne, C. and Weiss, P., Eds. Cambridge, MA: Harvard University Press.

Purao, S. (2002). Truth or Dare: Design Research in Information Technology, Working Paper. http://purao.ist.psu.edu/working-papers/dare-purao.pdf.

Takeda, H., Veerkamp, P., Tomiyama, T., and Yoshikawam, H. (1990). Modeling Design Processes. AI Magazine, 11(4), 37–48.

Trystam, J. (1971). From Automatic Documentation to the Data Bank. International Social Science Journal, 23(2), 285–293.

Vaishnavi, V. and Kuechler, W. (2004). Design Research in Information Systems. ISWorld. Updated January 20, 2006, http://www.isworld.org/Researchdesign/drisISworld.htm.

Chapter 4

A Process to Reuse Experiences via Written Narratives among Software Project Managers:

A Design Science Research Proposal

Stacie Petter

[Editorial Preface: Many of the readers of this book are no doubt interested in either the initiation of a design science research project or the evaluation of design science research. In either case, having an actual design science research proposal as a template should prove quite useful. The proposal below, in a modified form, was submitted by the author (of this chapter) as her dissertation proposal to the

Computer Information Systems Department of Georgia State University. Based on this proposal, the author was accepted to the prestigious doctoral consortium of the International Conference on Information Systems (ICIS), 2005. The proposal was accepted by her dissertation committee and ultimately enacted, and the resulting dissertation successfully defended. As one reads the proposal, refer back to Figure 2.3 occasionally and try to see how the various phases of the GDC are foreshadowed in the proposal. Like all good design science research (DSR) proposals, the unique capabilities of the DSR methodology for iterative learning and refinement of the research question or questions are explicitly anticipated.

Research Problem

Software development project disasters make worldwide headlines, and organizations have lost billions of dollars due to poor project implementations (Nash, 2000). The $4 billion loss by the IRS due to the inability to integrate obsolete systems (Abbott, 2000) and the cancellation of the Taurus system after spending over £80 million by the London Stock Exchange (Drummond, 1996) are examples of notable software development failures. The Standish Group, a research advisory firm, reports that only a third of the more than 13,500 software development projects evaluated in the 2003 CHAOS report were successful, and half of the software development projects in their report are classified as challenged, meaning these projects experienced cost and budget overruns (Larkowski, 2003). While this statistic on the state of software project management is gloomy, the state of project management is improving. For example, in 1994, the success rate of projects was only 16 percent (Larkowski, 2003). Although the percentage of successful software projects has doubled in the past decade, organizations must continue to find ways to reduce or, preferably, eliminate unnecessary spending due to problems in software project management.

Project management is the use of knowledge, skills, tools, and techniques to perform activities related to a temporary venture to develop a unique product or service according to stakeholder specifications (Project Management Institute, 2004). Project management is complex due to limited time, restricted capital, and high degrees of uncertainty during projects (Keil, 1999). There are several activities a project manager should perform to appropriately manage a project; however, most of the project management activities identified by Keil (1999), which also apply to software project management, emphasize the importance of planning projects. The best-planned projects, however, must be monitored and controlled and are still subject to problems (Project Management Institute, 2004). Deviations from the project plan often occur while executing software projects, and the project manager is responsible for ensuring that the project meets schedule, budget, functionality, and quality targets (Banker and Kemerer, 1992).

Although improvements to software project management have occurred through research, technology, and the efforts of professional organizations, more work should be done. Much of the previous research on software project management focused on planning projects, rather than on monitoring and controlling them. Although research on project planning is both important and necessary, less research has examined how to assist software project managers in controlling a software project. Controlling a project requires monitoring and adjusting the project plan to address deviations in schedule and budget, but controlling can also enable the project manager to anticipate and prevent future problems (Project Management Institute, 2004). The difficulty in controlling software projects is often caused by the need to manage multiple (and possibly conflicting) stakeholders and goals, handle ambiguous requirements, and integrate a team of individuals with different backgrounds (Kirsch, 1996); therefore, this less-examined aspect of software project management deserves further exploration.

Software project management is comprised of many knowledge-intensive activities such as planning, decision making, and problem solving, which are typically complicated and ill-structured (Grupe et al., 1998). Valuable knowledge gained before, during, and after the completion of projects is rarely captured and utilized across the organization (Schindler and Eppler, 2003). Reinvention of solutions, repetition of mistakes, and loss of process knowledge after project completion are knowledge-related problems that frequently occur during the execution of projects. These problems transpire due to turnover of project managers, failure to capture and reuse knowledge throughout and after the project, and insufficient technology to integrate knowledge with extant project management software (Tiwana and Ramesh, 2001). Organizations can have consistently successful projects by developing "an effective means of 'learning from experiences' on projects" (Cooke-Davies, 2002). Much of the prior research attempting to leverage knowledge from past projects, however, focused on measuring and using quantitative metrics for project planning and control. Metrics are necessary for planning a software development project and provide value while monitoring the progress of the project (DeMarco, 1982), yet focusing exclusively on metrics neglects a valuable type of knowledge, experiences shared among project managers via storytelling through written narratives or spoken folklore. The art of storytelling has proved a powerful method to enact change in organizations, such as the World Bank (Denning, 2000) and Xerox (Brown, 2001), and therefore narratives or stories could be useful in communicating project management experiences. Therefore, this research focuses on identifying, capturing, and reusing experiences of project management successes and failures in the form of written narratives to assist project managers when controlling software projects.

Research Questions

The purpose of this research is to create a process to assist software project managers in reusing past experiences. Thus, the general research question is as follows:

> What process can software project managers follow to reuse experiences in the form of written narratives to better address problems that arise when controlling a software project?

To answer this question, additional research questions also need answers, including:

- How do project managers reuse knowledge, such as their own or others' past experiences, when controlling a project?
- How can the decision-making process used by software project managers when controlling a project be augmented by experiences expressed in the form of written narratives — creating a *knowledge-based process*?
- Using the created knowledge-based process:
  - Are software project managers willing to adopt and use past experiences, in the form of narratives, within the knowledge-based process to efficiently and effectively share knowledge?
  - Are software project managers able to extract the knowledge within the experiences and apply it to a problem?
  - Does it improve the project manager's perception of his or her abilities?

Research Motivation

Project managers have tools available to share knowledge across projects in an effort to improve processes and decisions on future projects, yet many problems exist with the current methods of cross-project learning (Newell, 2004). For example, post-mortem analysis enables one to document lessons learned from projects; however, these lessons may not be disseminated and used throughout the organization if the lessons learned are complex in nature (Williams, 2004). Knowledge management systems, which "make the knowledge inside people's heads…widely available" (Swan et al., 1999), is another tool that software project managers can use to leverage knowledge from other projects. Building a knowledge repository alone, however, does not imply that people will actually use the knowledge within the repository (Davenport and Prusak, 2000). The reasons organizations implement these tools is their concern that knowledge is lost after project completion when team members move on to other activities or projects (Schindler and Eppler, 2003). The need to retain knowledge and lessons learned from projects is important to organizations (Schindler and Eppler, 2003); however, the current tools often are not promoting cross-project learning as intended (Newell, 2004).

Knowledge is a combination of experience, values, contextual information, and insight used to create a framework to evaluate and absorb new experiences and information (Davenport and Prusak, 2000). It is through a variety of experiences and learning-by-doing that one has the capability to create knowledge (Nonaka, 1994). Experience is essentially "what we have done and what has happened to us in the past" and is a critical component in developing knowledge as one uses experience to connect the past to the present (Davenport and Prusak, 2000). Experiences may be deeply personal or can be communicated through storytelling (Denning, 2000), mentoring (Swap et al., 2001), and documentation (Roth and Kleiner, 1998) in an effort to share one's knowledge with others.

One of the keys to managing a successful software project is an experienced project manager, yet many software project managers lack experience and key project management skills (Standish Group, 2001). Project managers often rely on their own past experiences to make decisions to keep the project on schedule, budget, functionality, and quality targets, yet these experiences are rarely shared among project managers (Schindler and Eppler, 2003). Furthermore, a problem that many software project managers face is their own lack of experience in managing software projects. Individuals may be promoted to the position of software project manager because of their ability to write code or lead a small development team; however, this experience alone is not enough to guarantee success as a software project manager (Standish Group, 2001). Organizations understand the importance of experience and often choose to hire individuals based on experience rather than academic training (Davenport and Prusak, 2000). Yet, while organizations may make these decisions in hiring new employees, individuals promoted from within the organization may lack critical experience in project management. For project managers with limited experience, it is possible to give them the benefits of the experiences of others in using methods such as mentoring or storytelling (Swap et al., 2001). Even for project managers with extensive experience, there is still the opportunity to learn from others when addressing a unique problem (Newell, 2004). Therefore, this research seeks to determine how to share experiences via written narratives among project managers for reuse in software projects.

Prior research acknowledges the ability to reuse knowledge across software projects, yet much of this research focuses exclusively on the use of metrics or seeks to enable reuse of knowledge among software developers rather than software project managers. The proposed research seeks to improve the reuse of a specific type of knowledge among software project managers, that is, experiences. This research focuses on reusing qualitative experiences rather than quantitative metrics, which has received less attention in the literature. Project management methods that use metrics are important and useful for software project management; however, focusing on metrics alone prevents the reuse of lessons learned across projects, which are often qualitative in nature. Narratives, which are qualitative, are considered one of the best methods to communicate knowledge because of the ability to develop a rich context of an event through the articulation of thoughts, feelings, and emotions

(Davenport and Prusak, 2000). Children listen to folklore and fairy tales because they are entertaining; parents and caregivers share these stories, often because of the lessons communicated through the narrative. It is possible to codify narratives and share them with others without losing value and meaning (Davenport and Prusak, 2000). The human interest for storytelling and the valuable knowledge that can be encoded in narratives suggest that sharing experiences via written narratives could be a powerful method to share knowledge among software project managers.

Research Approach

This research uses design science methodology to address the research questions posed in a prior section ("Research Problem"). Design science research is sometimes called "improvement research," and this designation emphasizes the problem-solving and performance-improving nature of the activity. While explanation research seeks to produce theoretical knowledge, design science research aims to "produce and apply knowledge of tasks or situations in order to create effective artifacts" to improve practice (March and Smith, 1995).

Takeda et al. (1990) have analyzed the reasoning that occurs in the course of a general design cycle of software. Vaishnavi and Kuechler (2004) have extended this analysis to explicate the knowledge generated in a design effort and apply the cycle specifically to information systems design science research leading to the general design cycle framework illustrated in Figure 4.1 (also see the section entitled "Overview of Design Science Research" in Chapter 2). In this framework, all design begins with Awareness of a Problem. Suggestions for a problem solution are abductively drawn from the existing knowledge or theory base for the problem area (Pierce, 1931) or developed using an appropriate research methodology. Next, implementing an artifact according to the suggested solution is attempted, shown as Development in Figure 4.1. This phase is where creativity plays a major role. Partially or fully successful implementations are then Evaluated (according to the functional specification implicit or explicit in the suggestion) on the goodness and effectiveness of the solution. Development, Evaluation, and further Suggestion are frequently performed iteratively in the course of the research (design) effort. The Circumscription arrow, or basis of the iteration, represents the flow from partial completion of the cycle back to Awareness of the Problem. Conclusion indicates termination of a specific design research project. The development of the framework shown in Figure 4.1 as the cognitive underpinning of information systems design science research (Hevner et al., 2004) is developed fully in Vaishnavi and Kuechler (2004).

Research Methodology

The research approach leverages design science research and follows the general design cycle described by Vaishnavi and Kuechler (2004). The final output of the

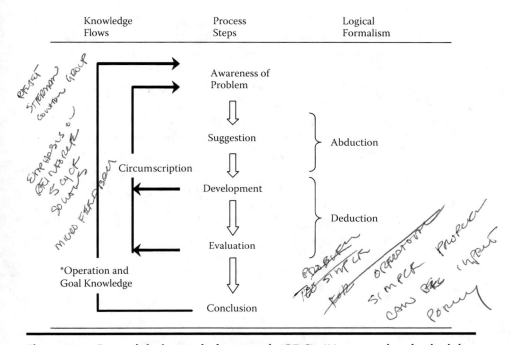

Figure 4.1 General design cycle framework (GDC). (*An operational principle can be defined as "any technique or frame of reference about a class of artifacts or its characteristics that facilitates creation, manipulation and modification of artifactual forms" (Dasgupta, 1996; Purao, 2002).)

research is a process of experience reuse that software project managers can leverage when performing tasks associated with controlling a project. This process can be instantiated in a support tool, such as a project methodology embedded in a software artifact, to encourage and promote experience reuse among software project managers within an organization.

The general design cycle (GDC) advocated by Vaishnavi and Kuechler (2004) also promotes the inclusion of multiple methods to inspire, generate, and evaluate an artifact via a design science research approach. The use of a multi-methodological research approach is not new to information systems research (Mingers, 2001) or, more specifically, information systems design science research, in that Nunamaker et al. (1991) advocated the benefits of using multiple methodologies via systems development research more than a decade ago.

Awareness of Problem

The first step of the GDC framework is an *awareness of a problem* through problem identification and definition. The problem identified in the current research is the difficulty in reusing experiences in the form of written narratives among software project managers when controlling a project. This research attempts to determine how to assist software project managers in avoiding the mistakes and repeating the successes previously made by others when performing tasks related to controlling a software project.

An often-neglected lesson is that researchers should spend "more time defining the problem before deciding to build a tool" (Parnas, 1998). In an effort to properly define the problem, a research sub-phase was identified and initiated to (1) determine that the problem has not been previously solved and determine what, if any, research has been previously performed in the area; (2) determine that the problem is widespread and that the solution will be an interesting contribution to the practice and academic communities; and (3) define and scope the problem as appropriate for the resources available to the project. After completing the research sub-phase, to ensure that the problem has not been previously solved, an evaluation of tools used by software project managers for leveraging knowledge was conducted. This evaluation provided further evidence that academic or practitioner communities have not previously solved the problem and offered inspiration for the continuation of the project.

Suggestion

Having identified the problem, research is necessary to derive *suggestions* to address the research problem. To examine the research question of how to facilitate the reuse of experiences among software project managers, it is important to gain an understanding of the current practices of project managers. Instead of relying solely on a literature review of knowledge management, project management, and decision making, which may not apply to software project managers who are asked to solve wicked problems under tremendous pressure (Grupe et al., 1998), an exploratory study will be conducted, in addition to a formal literature review, to examine how project managers search for knowledge and use experiences in a software project management context.

To examine how software project managers reuse experiences when making decisions in the control phase of software projects, the exploratory study will use grounded theory to identify a theory of knowledge reuse. Interviews with software project managers will be used to identify how knowledge is obtained and reused during a software project. The analysis will use grounded theory, which is a methodology that interweaves data generation and data analysis (Strauss and Corbin, 1990). Locke (1996) states that grounded theory "requires not only that data and theory be constantly compared and contrasted during data collection and analysis but also that the materializing theory drives ongoing data collection." In a grounded theory approach, the data generated is categorized and compared across observations. These observations are used to create theoretical statements. These theoretical statements then influence subsequent data generation, which will be categorized and compared. This recursive process will be used to inductively generate theoretical explanations about the phenomenon of knowledge reuse among software project managers.

Development

The *Awareness of the Problem* phase will determine what resources are available to software project managers for reusing knowledge and what gaps remain. The exploratory study in the *Suggestion* phase will provide a useful foundation for the creation of an artifact to encourage the reuse of experiences between software project managers. Furthermore, the literature will provide a guide regarding how to facilitate knowledge reuse via narratives between project managers. Equipped with the knowledge generated from prior research phases, the next question is how to utilize this knowledge, which leads to third phase, *Development*, in the GDC framework (Figure 4.1). This phase is where most of the actual *design* takes place, which is the creative effort required in synthesizing existing knowledge and a well-defined problem definition into an artifact for solving the problem. A resulting artifact of design science research may be rather abstract in nature, such as in the form of constructs, models, or methods (March and Smith, 1995). In the Development phase, the artifact's instantiation may be rather rudimentary because one focuses on design rather than the implementation of the artifact (Vaishnavi and Kuechler, 2004).

After gaining an understanding of the problem domain, and relevant theory and research (similar to eliciting requirements), one way to articulate this new-found knowledge is through a process specified by a conceptual model — an artifact of design science research (March and Smith, 1995). Conceptual modeling is a formal approach used by systems developers to better obtain and communicate requirements with stakeholders (Wand and Weber, 2002). Creating a conceptual model ensures that the requirements of such a process are fully understood. The goal of the current research is to examine *how* software project managers can better reuse experience. Using the conceptual model, an experience reuse process will be specified to illustrate an operationalization of how the conceptual model could be used in the software project management environment.

Evaluation

After the development of an artifact, it is necessary to evaluate the artifact using empirical methods "to determine *how well* an artifact works" (Hevner et al., 2004). There are multiple evaluation options, including action research, controlled experiments, simulation, or scenarios (Vaishnavi, 2004). In this research, an experiment will evaluate the artifact's utility. Experimentation is the chosen research methodology for the Evaluation phase due to its high internal validity and control (Whitley,

1996). This evaluation will examine if software project managers are willing *to adopt the process*, if *tacit knowledge can be extracted and applied* through the use of experiences, and if project managers have *a higher perception of their abilities* reflected by increased confidence and perceived quality of solutions to problems when using the process. As a result of this evaluation, future research (beyond the scope of this research proposal) will refine the conceptual model until a final experience reuse process is developed and evaluated.

Summary

This multi-methodological design science research approach benefits the field in that there are contributions that are relevant to both theory and practice at each stage of research. The Awareness of a Problem evaluation of current tools for knowledge reuse creates an understanding of what is currently available to project managers. The Suggestion phase provides a realization of what we can learn from existing research for solving the problem and an understanding of the current practices used by software project managers in reusing experiences to make decisions. The Development phase introduces an artifact that should provide practical benefit to practitioners and encourage more research regarding knowledge reuse and the role of experiences within the domain of project management. The Evaluation phase assesses the feasibility and effectiveness of the artifact and provides ideas for future research as the artifact is observed in the natural world. Figure 4.2 illustrates how the research phases map to the GDC framework.

Limitations and Expected Contributions

The proposed research has limitations. Although this research aims to create a useful artifact based on the evaluation of current tools used by project managers and the examination of current processes of software project managers in a single organization, it is possible that the created artifact may not be general enough to meet the needs of most project managers. Should this problem arise, future research should reexamine the Awareness of Problem and Suggestion phases of the general design cycle to ensure utility among a wider population of software project managers. A second limitation of this research is the narrow scope, which is experience reuse via written narratives for controlling software projects. This single aspect of software project management is important and warrants further research; however, due to the high degree of responsibility and lack of actual control a software project manager has over a project (Kirsch, 1997), the artifact may not have a high degree of impact on project success. However, if the developed artifact (the experience reuse process) is carefully designed, it may be possible to apply the process to other problems within software project management.

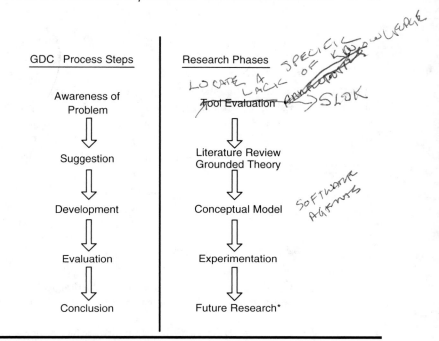

Figure 4.2   Mapping of general design cycle framework to research phases.

Although this research has limitations, it offers several contributions to research as well as practice. In terms of the research approach, this work is an exemplar of how design science research — and more specifically, the general design cycle — is an inclusive framework that uses multiple methodologies to address a research problem. Researchers often perceive design science research as addressing technical problems within the domain of information systems; however, this research uses design science research principles to address a practical and behavioral problem within software project management using multiple methodologies.

The exploratory, qualitative research (Suggestion phase) has a primary contribution of identifying current knowledge-reusing practices of software project managers with differing expertise. Much of the literature exploring the reuse of knowledge from past projects focuses on quantitative metrics rather than anecdotal evidence. Research has shown the benefits of using narratives and anecdotes to promote learning within a community, and these principles are examined within the software project management community.

By understanding the methods currently used by software project managers to reuse past experiences in making decisions during the controlling processes of software projects, one then has the potential to suggest improvements in the process. By identifying patterns or theory based on grounded theory research, design science research principles will determine how to more effectively allow software project managers to leverage experiences to better address issues that arise during the controlling processes of a project. Rather than simply understanding the difficulties faced by project managers, the contribution of the Development phase is to take action to help project managers make critical decisions during a project.

The final research phase (Evaluation) will evaluate the effectiveness of the artifact derived in the prior phases of this study. If the artifact performs well in the Evaluation stage, the research questions have been successfully answered and the process can be disseminated to practice for further trials and research. If the artifact does not meet all of the objectives, data collected from this stage of research will be used to guide future research in modifying the artifact to meet the needs of practice.

References

Abbott, B. (2000). Software Failure Can Lead to Financial Catastrophe, InfoWorld, October 2, pp. 54, 67.

Banker, R. and Kemerer, C. (1992). Performance Evaluation Metrics for Information Systems Development: A Principal-Agent Model. Information Systems Research, 3(4), 379–400.

Brown, J. (2001). Xerox: How Copiers Actually Get Repaired, in Storytelling: Passport to Success in the 21st Century. S. Kahan, Ed. http://www.johnseelybrown.com/seth_int.html.

Cooke-Davies, T. (2002). The "Real" Success Factors on Projects. International Journal of Project Management, 20(3), 185–190.

Dasgupta, S. (1996). Technology and Creativity. New York: Oxford University Press.

Davenport, T. and Prusak, L. (2000). Working Knowledge: How Organizations Manage What They Know (paperback edition). Boston, MA: Harvard Business School Press.

DeMarco, T. (1982). Controlling Software Projects. New York: Yourdon Press, p. 284.

Denning, S. (2000). The Springboard: How Storytelling Ignites Action in Knowledge-Era Organizations. Woburn, MA: Butterworth-Heinemann, p. 248.

Drummond, H. (1996). The Politics of Risk: Trials and Tribulations of the Taurus Project. Journal of Information Technology, 11(4), 347–357.

Grupe, F., Urwiler, R., Ramarapu, N., and Owrang, M. (1998). The Application of Case-Based Reasoning to the Software Development Process. Information and Software Technology, 40(9), 493–499.

Hevner, A., March, S., Park, J., and Ram, S. (2004). Design Science in Information Systems Research. MIS Quarterly, 28(1), 75–105.

Keil, M. (1999). Project Management, in Wiley Encyclopedia of Electrical and Electronics Engineering, Webster, J.G., Ed. New York: Kim H. Kelly, pp. 384–397.

Kirsch, L.J. (1996). The Management of Complex Tasks in Organizations: Controlling the Systems Development Process. Organization Science, 7(1), 1–21.

Kirsch, L.J. (1997). Portfolios of Control Modes and IS Project Management. Information Systems Research, 8(3), 215–239.

Larkowski, K. (2003). Latest Standish Group CHAOS Report Shows Project Success Rates Have Improved by 50%. West Yarmouth, MA: Standish Group International, p. 1.

Locke, K. (1996). Rewriting The Discovery of Grounded Theory After 25 Years. Journal of Management Inquiry, 5(3), 239–245.

March, J. (1991). Exploration and Exploitation in Organizational Learning. Organization Science, 2(1), 71–87.

March, S and Smith, G. (1995). Design and Natural Science Research on Information Technology. Decision Support Systems, 15, 251–266.

Mathiassen, L., Robertson, M., and Swan, J. (2003). Cracking the Code: The Dynamics of Professional Knowledge. European Knowledge Management Conference, Barcelona, Spain.

May, D. and Taylor, P. (2003). Knowledge Management with Patterns. Communications of the ACM, 67(4), 94–99.

Mingers, J. (2001). Combining IS Research Methods: Towards a Pluralist Methodology. Information Systems Research, 12(3), 240–259.

Nash, K. (2000). Companies Don't Learn from Previous IT Snafus. ComputerWorld, 32–33, 36.

Newell, S. (2004). Enhancing Cross-Project Learning. Engineering Management Journal, 16(1), 12–20.

Nonaka, I. (1994). A Dynamic Theory of Organizational Knowledge Creation. Organization Science, 5(1) 14–37.

Nonaka, I. and Takeuchi, H. (1995). The Knowledge Creating Company. New York: Oxford University Press.

Nunamaker, J., Jay F., Chen, M., and Purdin, T.P.M. (1991). Systems Development in Information Systems Research, Journal of Management Information Systems, 7(3), 89–106.

Parnas, D. (1998). Who Taught Me about Software Engineering Research. Software Engineering Notes, 23(4), 26–28. Cambridge, MA: Harvard University Press.

Project Management Institute, A Guide to the Project Management Body of Knowledge (PMBOK Guide), third edition. Newburn Square, PA: Project Management Institute, 2004.

Purao, S. (2002). Truth or Dare: Design Research in Information Technology. GSU Department of CIS Working Paper. Atlanta, GA.

Roth, G. and Kleiner, A. (1998). Developing Organizational Memory through Learning Histories. Organizational Dynamics, Autumn, pp. 43–60.

Schindler, M. and Eppler, M.J. Harvesting Project Knowledge: A Review of Project Learning Methods and Success Factors. International Journal of Project Management, 21(3), 219–228.

Standish Group (2001). Extreme CHAOS. West Yarmouth, MA: The Standish Group International, Inc., p. 12.

Strauss, A. and Corbin, J. (1990). Basics of Qualitative Research, Newbury Park, CA: Sage Publications, Inc.

Swan, J., Newell, S., Scarborough, H., and Hislop, D. (1999). Knowledge Management and Innovation: Networks and Networking, Journal of Knowledge Management, 3(4), 262.

Swap, W., Leonard, D., Shields, M., and Abrams, L. (2001). Using Mentoring and Storytelling to Transfer Knowledge in the Workplace. Journal of Management Information Systems, 18(1), 95–114.

Takeda, H., Veerkamp, P., Tomiyama, T., and Yoshikawa, H. (1990). Modeling Design Processes. AI Magazine, pp. 37–48.

Tiwana, A. and Ramesh, B. (2001). A Design Knowledge Management System to Support Collaborative Information Product Evolution. Decision Support Systems, 31(2), 241–262.

Vaishnavi, V. and Kuechler, W. (2004). Design Research in Information Systems. ISWorld, Atlanta, GA, http://www.isworld.org/Researchdesign/drisISworld.htm. Accessed December 30, 2006.

Vaishnavi, V. (2004). Research Patterns: Improving and Innovating Information Systems and Technology. Version 1.0, 2004. Georgia State University, Atlanta, GA.

Wand, Y. and Weber, R. (2002). Information Systems and Conceptual Modeling — A Research Agenda. Information Systems Research, 13(4), December, 363–376.

Whitley, B.E. (1996). Behavioral Science: Theory, Research, and Application, in: Principles of Research in Behavioral Science, Mountain View, CA: Mayfield Publishing, pp. 1–30.

Williams, T. (2004). Identifying the Hard Lessons from Projects — Easily. International Journal of Project Management, 22(4), 273–279.

II

PATTERNS

Chapter 5

Using Patterns to Illuminate Research Practice

Introduction

This chapter describes patterns from several perspectives: first their historical origin as a means of communicating architectural design themes, and then as they are used in this book to describe aspects of the *art* of design science research. The general design cycle (GDC) is then revisited (from previous chapters), adapted specifically for use as a framework for understanding design science research projects. The chapter concludes with an extended case study of the use of patterns in the same development project — of the Smart Object Paradigm — recounted in narrative in Chapter 2.

Patterns, Then and Now

Patterns, as we use the term here, is a communication technique developed and first used by Christopher Alexander (1964) to communicate a *way of building* structures to his architecture students. Alexander's intent was not to communicate facts about structures — how to calculate the loading on a specific type of stair, for example

— but rather to convey the much more subtle skill (or art) of constructing structures whose components flowed gracefully and meaningfully into one another to create a coherent design. Some of the problems inherent in trying to communicate this type of knowledge are visible in the word usage that describes the result: what does it mean for components to flow? Even more, what does it mean for them to flow gracefully and meaningfully? Finally, what is a "coherent" design? A time-honored answer to such questions is: Let me show you an example. In a literal sense, patterns are a language-based way to communicate let-me-show-you-an-example. They are similar to but shorter and more structured than the case studies used to communicate similarly subtle and impossible-to-precisely-pin-down knowledge in business classes.

Patterns are also frequently defined as "a solution to a problem in a recurring context." However, the context for the type of problems patterns best address is never identical and so patterns are typically goal based rather than strictly algorithmic. A pattern demonstrates a way to, or general technique for, approaching a class or type of problems that are abstractly similar to other problems although they have never occurred before in exactly the same way. Patterns are almost never presented as a set of strict rules because precision always limits applicability.* At this point, our ability to describe patterns with more words has been exhausted and thus we too now fall back on examples.

As discussed in Chapter 2, research is an at-best-semi-structured activity. This is true in part because the nature of the activity is to explore the unknown, that is, the unstructured. A common problem when pursuing research in an interesting but new-to-you area is to become overwhelmed by the new information you have gathered, which, by definition, is only generally applicable to an area not well understood by anyone and especially not by you. Place yourself in that problem; most researchers, however new, have had this experience — try to recall that feeling as vividly as possible. Now turn to the pattern on page 105 of this book: *Structuring an Ill-Structured Problem*. Does it provide any assistance? Does it provide at least a high-level ordering-principle? For further assistance with the same problem, read carefully the pattern on page 107 of this book, *Complex System Analysis*. Notice that the patterns focus your attention on a specific aspect of a situation without being task specific. They use phrases such as "analyze the structure..." without specifying what they mean by analysis or structure. In this way they are able to focus your vast store of tacit knowledge (or "common sense").

---

* A textbook in artificial intelligence from the second author's graduate study (Firebaugh, 1988) contained a "quantitative" version of the precision-limits-applicability truism that is applicable here: Generality * Utility = C (a constant). That is, one can make a concept or artifact more immediately useful only by making it more specific and thus limiting its generality. Conversely, the general applicability of a concept or artifact can be increased only by abstracting it and decreasing its utility in any specific context.

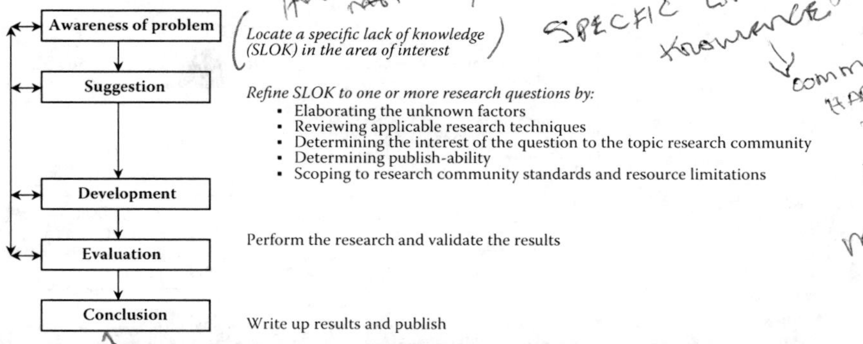

Awareness of problem — (Locate a specific lack of knowledge (SLOK) in the area of interest)

Suggestion — *Refine SLOK to one or more research questions by:*
- Elaborating the unknown factors
- Reviewing applicable research techniques
- Determining the interest of the question to the topic research community
- Determining publish-ability
- Scoping to research community standards and resource limitations

Development

Evaluation — Perform the research and validate the results

Conclusion — Write up results and publish

Figure 5.1 The general design cycle (GDC) adapted for design science research.

The General Design Cycle Revisited

Figure 5.1 is a "roadmap" for a design science research project: a general, iterative research model with patterns applicable to each phase or stage. This is an elaboration on the general design cycle (GDC) and on the design science research (DSR) methodology presented in Chapter 2.

The arrows out of and into every phase of Figure 5.1 indicate that the method is indefinitely iterative. At any phase prior to (a satisfactory) conclusion, it is possible and sometimes necessary to return to an earlier phase. This is the nature of creative thought in general and design in particular; examples of iteration between phases are given in the extended description of the authors' design research project given in Chapter 2 ("An Example of ICT Design Science Research"). As also discussed in Chapter 2, the iterative nature of the method makes possible the generation of circumscription knowledge not possible without iteration.

The methodology and the patterns are quite general; however, they make several assumptions that we now make explicit:

1. *Interest in the area of investigation.* While the intent of many of the patterns is to help narrow the scope of research (*Research Domain Identification, Problem Formulation*) or align it more closely with a community of research or practice (*Understanding Research Community, Research Conversation, Industry/Practice Awareness*), we assume you have chosen an area in which you already have a general interest.
2. *A desire to publish.* This assumption follows closely from the assumption of genuine interest in an area. We assume the research is intended to produce new knowledge that you and some community will consider valuable and interesting and that you will wish to share the knowledge through publication.

Figure 5.1 has been modified as Figure 5.2, in which the patterns applicable to each phase of the methodology are indicated by their name and the number of the chapter in which they are found adjacent to each phase. If

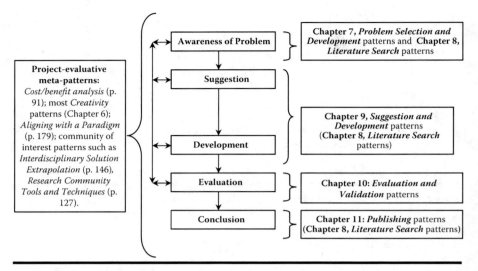

Figure 5.2 Patterns applicable at various phases of the design research design cycle.

you are reading the CD-ROM of the online version of this book, each pattern designation is a link to the page describing the pattern and the beginning of the applicable chapter.

The categorization scheme chosen for the patterns corresponds to the major activities of a design research project when the project is viewed as a work process. The categories are used as the chapter headings of the current part (Part II) of the book in which the patterns are described in detail:

Creativity (Chapter 6)
Problem Selection and Development (Chapter 7)
Literature Search (Chapter 8)
Suggestion and Development (Chapter 9)
Evaluation and Validation (Chapter 10)
Publishing (Chapter 11)

Creativity patterns (Chapter 6) are applicable to all the phases of the research project. The patterns in Chapters 7 and 8 are applicable to the Awareness of Problem phase of the project. The patterns in Chapter 9 are applicable to two phases of the research project: Suggestion and Development. Patterns in Chapters 10 and 11 are applicable to the Evaluation and Conclusion phases of the project, respectively. In addition, patterns in Chapter 8 are also useful in the Suggestion and Conclusion phases of the research project.

Note also that many of the patterns appear adjacent to multiple methodology phases and that some have notation indicating applicability across the methodology as a whole. This is because different patterns operate at different levels of abstraction. For example, the patterns on creativity (Chapter 6) are applicable at any point in the research process when progress is stalled for want of ideas. By contrast, the *Familiarization with New Area* pattern (page 111) is applicable primarily at the Awareness of Problem stage or the Suggestion stage. We refer henceforward to the most broadly applicable patterns as *meta-level* patterns. Due to its generality (as opposed to its level), a given pattern may be applicable at multiple stages in the methodology. This is strength of patterns but it can be confusing: some patterns are context independent, and it is up to the user to supply the context and details of the usage suggested by the pattern.

A case illustrating the use of patterns in an actual design science research project is presented below to make the concepts concrete and situate them in their use context by showing the actions that resulted from their application. Because it is the case with which we have the most familiarity, we will revisit the Smart Object development project, discussed in Chapter 2 ("An Example of ICT Design Science Research") to illustrate the general design cycle itself.

Pattern Usage in the Development of the Smart Object Paradigm

Please review the section in Chapter 2 entitled "An Example of ICT Design Science Research" in this book prior to reading the pattern use discussion. That section gave the story line for the case and covers many details that are not repeated here. The use of patterns described below follows the narrative in the cited section in Chapter 2 and follows the general design science research cycle of Figures 5.1 and 5.2. The designed artifact in this case is the research project itself. The multiple goals for the project include:

1. Determine a problem interesting to one or more design science research communities.
2. Scope the problem to available resources while maintaining its "interestingness."
3. Solve the problem (improve the problem situation) with a designed artifact, that is, design and implement the artifact.
4. Evaluate the artifact.
5. Publish the results of the study.

The problems that arose in the pursuit of these goals and the patterns that were used to approach and overcome those problems are discussed in detail in the following section.

Pre-Awareness of Problem

The broadest context in which to consider the case and the application of patterns is the academic setting in which it took place. There is an intellectual restlessness in any Ph.D. granting institution (in this case, Georgia State University), and it arises from two sources: (1) the high native levels of interest in certain subject areas in the people who self-select to such environments and (2) the pragmatic search for *interesting* problems to *solve* and their explication *published.* (Publication influences compensation in the academic environment of many countries including the United States.) The following discussion exposes the meta-level use of research patterns that are operable even before the problem identification and (problem) awareness stages of the general design methodology. Indeed, these patterns are constantly applicable in the academic environment and literally shape the Awareness stage (Searle, 1995).

First, consider the adjectives "interesting" and "published" when applied to the word "problem." At any point in time, design science research (or any broad type of research) is found interesting and publishable by only a limited number of communities of interest and their journals. Further, design science research itself is applicable only to a certain class of problem domains (defined, somewhat circularly, by the communities that use the paradigm).

The *Aligning with a Paradigm* and *Research Domain Identification* patterns were first applied in this case *unconsciously* as part of the environmental scanning mode of the researchers. The principal actors were an experienced design science researcher and an apprentice design science researcher. The domains of interest and possible publication outlets were generally known, the various paradigms applicable to design science research were also familiar at a high level, and this information served as a preconscious filter, selecting for conscious-attention only design science research opportunities (Gladwell, 2005). For example, it would never have occurred to Vijay Vaishnavi (or later to Gary Buchanan) to pursue an opportunity for research on *organizational structural change following IT deployment* because problems from this area neither "fit" the design science research paradigm nor are they one of the paradigm's research domains.

However, for someone new to design science research, *Aligning with a Paradigm* and *Research Domain Identification* will be valuable guides for becoming familiar with design science research methods, problems, and journals. *Aligning with a Paradigm, Research Conversation,* and *Research Domain Identification* each involve extensive, reflective *reading* from the work of a research community, or direct observation of its work and then consideration of a course of action in light of the values revealed for that community. The patterns explicate and direct the time-honored advice to *become familiar with your research community.* In this case, familiarization with a community had been largely accomplished over a prior period of years and resulted in the selective perception (Kunda, 1987) used (pre-consciously) to scan the environment for interesting problem domains.

Awareness of Problem

The opportunity that passed the filter put in place by the meta-level use of the three patterns discussed above and that initiated this case was a chance to investigate the command and control difficulties that arose in a critically complex environment, that of nuclear reactors. Following an invitation from a colleague at Georgia Tech (GT), Vaishnavi and several other Georgia State faculty members made several tours of the GT research reactor. Between tours, the following patterns were applied:

- The meta-level patterns discussed above — *Aligning with a Paradigm, Research Conversation,* and *Research Domain Identification* — were reapplied at a more concrete level. First, it was necessary to establish that the problem set presented by nuclear reactor command and control was amenable to exploration by design science research (*Aligning with a Paradigm*). This seemed to be so; IT systems with embedded control paradigms and expert system modules were in use, and improvement of these systems constituted a partial solution of the overall problem. Such improvement was definitely part of the DSR paradigm. Notice how the general research direction (IT control system improvement) arose from the use of a very general pattern, very early in the case.
- Next, it was necessary to identify the research domains and specific research conversations implied by the problem domain. This information was identified through focused library research guided by the following patterns: *Problem Area Identification, Problem Formulation, Understanding Research Community,* and *Research Conversation.* (Note: Many of these patterns will be used again later as the research problem and its solution become more focused.)

After tours of the reactor facility and follow-up question sessions of reactor personnel by phone and meetings, Vaishnavi had amassed a substantial quantity of information. The *Problem Area Identification, Complex System Analysis, Problem Formulation, Understanding Research Community, Research Conversation,* and *Research Domain Identification* patterns were applied to attempt to identify a more specific and more tightly scoped problem. However, there was need to move to the next stage (Suggestion) to develop a preliminary solution and to see its shortcomings before a well-scoped research problem could be defined. This shows the need for iteration between the different phases of the research. Table 5.1 summarizes the use of all patterns in this phase of research.

Suggestion

The Suggestion phase of DSR involves utilizing information gained in scanning the literature using *Literature Search* and *Brainstorming* to investigate potential avenues of approach to the problem. Following the application of the *Industry and Practice*

Table 5.1   Pattern Application during the Awareness of Problem Phase of Research

Patterns Utilized	Actions Generated
Aligning with a Paradigm (p. 179); Research Conversation (p. 88); and Research Domain Identification (p. 84)	Using these patterns, a design research opportunity emerged from a serendipitous site visit to an interesting (of and about designed artifacts) site.
Problem Area Identification (p. 86); Complex System Analysis (p. 107); Problem Formulation (p. 87); Understanding Research Community (p. 112); Research Conversation (p. 88); Research Domain Identification (p. 84)	Using these patterns, opportunities for IT-related improvement of the operation of the site were investigated and a preliminary problem determined. The appropriate research community — complex control systems design — was identified.
Industry and Practice Awareness (p. 116); Research Conversation (p. 88); Solution and Scope Mismatch (p. 93); Being Visionary (p. 95); Brainstorming (p. 79); Problem Formulation (p. 87)	When applied to what had been discovered of the problem domain given the effort expended to date, these patterns suggested that the domain was ill defined, and simply determining a properly scoped ("do-able") problem would be challenging. This phase of the project was revisited after developing a preliminary solution in the Suggestion phase and a more tightly defined research problem formulated.
Bridging Research Communities (p. 98); Research Domain Identification (p. 84); Understanding Research Community (p. 112); Research Conversation (p. 88)	Three distinct but interrelated research communities were identified, and the literature for the research communities was revisited in a focused manner via the application of these patterns.

Awareness, Problem Space Tools and Techniques, and *Research Community Tools and Techniques* patterns, it initially seemed that an approach widely successful in other, superficially familiar environments, expert system design, might prove useful in this case. The second major actor in the case, Gary Buchanan, a doctoral student at Georgia State, was brought into the project to develop an expert system in PRO-LOG for use in controlling the reactor. However, the application of several other patterns uncovered problems with the first-pass solution, including:

■ *Cost-Benefit Analysis* is another pattern that can be applied at multiple levels. In this case, after several weeks of development, the slow rate of progress on the project became apparent. More detailed analysis of the problem and application of the *Solution-Scope Mismatch* pattern showed that the available methods of expert system development were inadequate to a problem of this scale.

■ *Means-Ends Analysis* showed that the primary problem was not in modeling the control rules, but rather in determining when many apparently similar rules should be applied. The *General Solution Principle* and *Abstracting Concepts* patterns helped Vaishnavi and Buchanan proceed toward a solution that was broader, more generally applicable, and more elegant than would have been likely otherwise. This pattern advises rethinking potential solutions to encompass more and more aspects of the problem. In this specific case, this pattern caused Vaishnavi and Buchanan to reject more ad-hoc solutions such as development of an expert system design tool and focus instead on conceiving something that better modeled complex command structures in general.

The Awareness of Problem phase was revisited and using the *Industry/Practice Awareness, Research Conversation, Solution-Scope Mismatch, Being Visionary, Brainstorming*, and *Problem Formulation* patterns, the research problem was redefined. At this stage, the general problem — how to construct and continuously maintain a support system for the operation of a complex, hierarchical procedure driven environment — became explicit and remained the focus of the project through its completion. Three interrelated research areas — software engineering, database systems, and knowledge-based systems — were identified as areas that have dealt with modeling complex systems. The problem of bridging these areas was identified using the *Bridging Research Communities* pattern. The literature for these areas was revisited and analyzed. Table 5.1 summarizes the additional patterns used in the Awareness of Problem phase.

By this point in the project, both Vaishnavi and Buchanan felt they were "onto something"; that is, they felt the problem was interesting and potentially solvable. This was an intuitive feeling, one of the aspects of research in general that cannot be completely captured with patterns, but that can be partially validated through the use of patterns such as *Research Conversation* that lead to actions that demonstrate alignment with a community for both problem and solution domains.

Means-Ends Analysis suggested that rule-based control systems were theoretically appropriate but practically unmanageable with existing techniques. Scrutinizing the results from the effort to date using *Cost-Benefit Analysis* — only a general solution direction had emerged at this point — indicated that even a partial solution to the problem would likely involve considerable work. At this point, Buchanan decided to pursue the problem as his dissertation topic.

The *Research Conversation* pattern and other literature search patterns were used continuously throughout this phase. This uncovered an interesting in-use technique that seemed promising: frame-based knowledge representation in which multiple, similar aspects of a domain and rules for responding to them were encapsulated in a frame. Through the use of the *Sketching Solution* pattern, a frame-based approach was investigated as a thought experiment. *Complex System Analysis* followed by *Means-Ends Analysis* found this approach also lacking; frames, as understood at that time, suffered from the same maintenance problems as simple rule-based systems.

In the course of an extended "gestation period" (also in the authors' experience, a facet of all research), the *Brain Storming, Different Perspectives, Integrating Techniques,* and *Combining Partial Solutions* patterns were applied repeatedly to investigate different approaches to the problem. The approaches were evaluated using the *Sketching Solution* and *Means-Ends Analysis* patterns. After many iterations through solution proposal and solution evaluation that spanned several months, the application of object-oriented (OO) programming techniques seemed promising; if rules could be encapsulated in objects, then the inheritance and especially the reuse capabilities of the OO paradigm could possibly be leveraged to ameliorate the problem of rule maintenance that characterized the problem domain. More thought experiments guided by the *Sketching Solution* and *Means-Ends Analysis* patterns showed this approach, a direct result of applying the *Integrating Techniques* and *Combining Partial Solutions* patterns, to be promising. Having identified an approach to the problem, the next phase of the general design method (i.e., Development) was initiated. Table 5.2 summarizes all the patterns applied and resulting actions during the Suggestion phase.

Development

Development involves in-depth exploration, development, and assessment of a solution direction. It requires the repeated suggestion of methods for specifically how to accomplish the solution, turning a solution direction into a solution-in-fact. It is necessarily iterative for almost all nontrivial problems because large, imperfectly understood problems (by definition, the "interesting" problems for researchers) are multifaceted, with each facet typically explored and tentatively solved in turn. However, all facets must integrate into a coherent whole if they are to provide an acceptable solution and thus backtracking to reassess a prior partial solution that impedes solution of another facet is common.

Because the chosen approach was a synthesis of rule-based and object-oriented programming (from the *Integrating Techniques* and *Elegant Design* patterns), the preliminary design step seemed obvious: substitute rules for programmed methods in a novel, OO language. The two patterns key to this design stage, *Sketching Solution* and *Means-Ends Analysis*, when applied to this facet of the solution showed it to be feasible but inadequate. The ability to inherit from previously defined objects offered some improvement over frames in maintaining large rule sets, but was still, as shown by thought experiments that "walked through" the use of these novel constructs, insufficient to manage the scale of the maintenance problem. The solution direction still seemed promising however, especially because application of

PROBLEM AWARENESS

Table 5.2 Pattern Application during the Suggestion Phase of Research

Patterns Utilized	Actions Generated
Industry and Practice Awareness (p. 116); Problem Space Tools and Techniques (p. 126); Research Community Tools and Techniques (p. 127)	When applied to what had been discovered of the problem domain given the effort expended to date, these patterns suggested that the domain was ill defined and simply determining a properly scoped ("do-able") problem would be challenging.
Brainstorming (p. 79); Research Conversation (p. 88); Complex System Analysis (p. 157)	These patterns were used to cycle through potentially interesting aspects of the total problem space using ongoing research conversations to suggest approaches.
Cost-Benefit Analysis (p. 91); Solution-Scope Mismatch (p. 93); Means/Ends Analysis (p. 156); General Solution Principle (p. 148); Abstracting Concepts (p. 150)	These patterns made clear the shortcomings of the preliminary solution and helped the more general and more interesting (to the research community) problem to emerge.
Sketching Solution (p. 139); Research Conversation (p. 88); Complex System Analysis (p. 107); Means-Ends Analysis (p. 156)	These patterns permitted (relatively) rapid development of and evaluation of approaches to the general problem of control of a complex, rapidly evolving environment.
Brainstorming (p. 79); Different Perspectives (p. 147); Integrating Techniques (p. 154); Combining Partial Solutions (p. 142); Sketching Solution (p. 139); Means-Ends Analysis (p. 156)	These patterns were responsible for the synthesis of rule-based systems with object-oriented concepts and the evaluation of this combined approach.

the *Hierarchical Design* pattern showed that the overall complexity of the environment could be partitioned and modeled — and potentially controlled — through this approach.

An aspect of design that is shared by any creative endeavor is the manner in which a continuing focus on a problem changes the perception of the issue. It becomes more clear and better articulated even as, or perhaps because, multiple solutions have been attempted and have been discarded. Each attempt broadens the conceptual vocabulary that can be used in the problem description. Application of the *Using Human Roles* pattern was natural to the project at this point because it is a common technique in OO design — describe in detail what a human would do to solve the problem and then use the *Being Visionary* pattern to conceive an automated approach to the human activities. The current, human approach was to use experience and judgment to select from the huge rule set an immediately applicable subset for different, superficially similar situations. At some point, the OO conception of "letting the objects direct themselves" became prominent and the most distinguishing feature of smart objects started to emerge: the use of a "judgment" or meta-level within and among objects containing rules sets to automate the selection of appropriate lower-level rules. Essentially, higher-level rules would simulate human intervention to automate the contextual selection of lower-level rule sets to be activated. The details of how the higher- and lower-level rules would interact were far from clear at this point; however, the broad applicability of the functional specification of this capability was powerful and elegant (*Elegant Design*).

Although the use of meta-level rules to guide rule-set selection had been suggested in the literature (continuing application of the *Understanding Research Community,* and *Interdisciplinary Solution, Extrapolation,* and *Research Conversation* patterns), the application and expansion of OO techniques provided a superior partitioning of and execution scheme for high-level rules than any technique yet discovered by Vaishnavi and Buchanan in their literature search. This tentative conclusion of the superiority of the new technique was, of course, immediately subjected to the *Sketching Solution* and *Means-Ends Analysis* patterns. Use of the *Theory Development* and *Approaches to Building Theory* patterns helped in developing and formalizing the theory developed. Table 5.3 summarizes the patterns applied and resulting actions during the Development phase.

Following the generation of a specific approach to the problem (a meta-level rule interpreter as a common part of all smart objects) came months of even lower-level implementation work to articulate the general constructs into software design modules capable of being implemented in an existing OO language.

Evaluation

As discussed in Chapter 2 ("An Example of ICT Design Science Research"), micro-evaluation of aspects of a design takes place almost constantly during the Suggestion and Development phases of the design cycle. However, in the Evaluation phase of the cycle, the goal is a macro-evaluation or validation of the entire designed artifact.

The smart object concept had many *theoretical* benefits and had proved feasible in the prior phase of the design cycle. Now it was time to empirically explore whether or not the design actually realized the theoretical benefits claimed for it. Design research is sometimes criticized for its lack of empirical validation. In this case, Buchanan and Vaishnavi were sensitive to this criticism and spent considerable time, guided by multiple patterns, to find an evaluation process for smart objects that was both rigorous enough to demonstrate the value of the concept and yet achievable with the resources available.

The *Technological Approach Exemplars* pattern led to another review of the problem domain literature, this time focused on discovering what validation techniques were used by the chosen research community. This information would not

Table 5.3 Pattern Application during the Development Phase of Research

Patterns Utilized	Actions Generated
Integrating Techniques (p. 154); Elegant Design (p. 132)	Suggested the synthesis of object-oriented and rule-based programming (smart objects) as a concrete means of solving the research problem.
Sketching Solution (p. 139); Means-Ends Analysis (p. 156)	Use of these patterns (1) developed the smart object synthesis more explicitly and (2) determined that the development was leading toward results at an acceptable pace.
Hierarchical Design (p. 136)	This pattern suggested still more elaboration of the smart object concept.
Using Human Roles (p. 153); Being Visionary (p. 95)	When combined with Hierarchical Design, these patterns resulted in conceptualization of one of the key aspects of the final smart object paradigm: the incorporation of a meta-level of supervisory rules to simulate the human intervention required by conventional solutions of the research problem.
Elegant Design (p. 132); Research Conversation (p. 88); Sketching Solution (p. 139); Means-Ends Analysis (p. 156); Interdisciplinary Solution Extrapolation (p. 146); Theory Development (p. 121); Approaches to Building Theory (p. 122)	Application of these patterns (1) confirmed that the smart object paradigm was a unique contribution, and (2) that it did in fact provide a solution to the general research problem, and in creating and presenting the theory developed.

absolutely constrain the direction taken, but would definitely influence it; it is widely understood that straying beyond the techniques commonly employed by a research community increases the difficulty of publishing in that community (Murray, 2005). It was discovered that literally all the techniques of evaluation and validation explored by the patterns in Chapter 9 of this book had been applied to different published DSR efforts and were acceptable to the DSR community. Thus, for this case, the actual choice of validation technique and its scope would have to be determined by the specifics of the project and by still another application of the pattern: *Cost-Benefit Analysis.*

A consideration of the *Mathematical Proofs* pattern made it apparent that formal proof was not applicable to smart objects. The artifact was a conceptual design from a potentially infinite design space and no approach to optimization has yet been developed. Likewise, preliminary use of the *Using Metrics* pattern showed that metrics were inapplicable because no formal metrics existed for evaluating the control of large, complex systems. Further, *Experimentation*, involving by definition the comparison of two or more control techniques when applied to the same environment, was eliminated as impractical given the resources available for the project. The reasoning involved in this decision merits further discussion.

As was discussed in Chapter 2 ("An Example of ICT Design Science Research"), researchers from other paradigms sometimes find the degree of validation applied to designed artifacts simplistic. This is due to the lack of understanding of the extraordinary difficulty of "full-scale" validation of a complex artifact, understanding that typically comes only from experience or long and close observation of the design process.

In this case, a "full-scale" test of the smart object paradigm as applied to a nuclear reactor environment would have involved man-years of effort, broken out as follows. First, a smart object interpreter or compiler would have needed to have been constructed and tested; the effort for this process alone was known from experience to be on the order of man-years. Next, it would have been necessary to design and program a full-scale control system in the new interpreter or compiler. Finally, it would have been necessary to install the control system at the nuclear reactor facility, train the full staff in its use, and operate the system over a period of time with extensive measurements and observations taken of all processes. Even a cursory application of the *Cost-Benefit Analysis* pattern indicated that the amount of effort required for a full-scale test of the smart object paradigm could not be justified for a single dissertation and the possibility of one or two publications.

Fortunately, the research communities of interest in this case were all design science research oriented and were amenable to more modest forms of validation than full-scale testing. Although some forms of validation had been ruled out by the nature of the project, the use of the *Technological Approach Exemplars* pattern led to the conjunction of the use of *Demonstration, Simulation,* and *Logical Reasoning* evaluation patterns. This yielded a validation strategy that was essentially an extended demonstration of the operation of smart objects at a logical level. The strategy had two stages: (1) the functional logic description of a smart object execution engine was reasoned to have the attributes claimed for the smart object design; and (2) the second stage involved an extended "walk-through" or detailed step-by-step explication of the logical operation of a smart object design for a simple robot executing the task of bagging groceries. Successful operation of this exercise would, at least for the research community consisting of Buchanan's dissertation committee, constitute proof of concept of a novel, useful advance in knowledge. Table 5.4 summarizes the patterns applied and resulting actions during the Evaluation phase.

Table 5.4 Pattern Application during the Evaluation Phase of Research

Patterns Utilized	Actions Generated
Technological Approach Exemplars (p. 155)	This pattern guided the researchers toward validation of techniques that were acceptable to the research community.
Mathematical Proofs (p. 170); Using Metrics (p. 166)	These patterns were used in a via negativa — a preliminary application demonstrated that the smart object paradigm was not amenable to these validation techniques.
Technological Approach Exemplars (p. 155); Demonstration (p. 160); Simulation (p. 164); Logical Reasoning (p. 168)	Technological Approach Exemplars served as a meta-level pattern, suggesting a validation strategy that incorporated the synergistic application of multiple patterns in validating the research.
Cost-Benefit Analysis (p. 91)	This pattern was applied specifically to the validation strategy as it emerged to ensure that resources were not exceeded. An artful balance was called for in creating a validation that satisfied Technological Approach Exemplars (and thus made publication easier) and the eternal problem of resource limitations.

Conclusion

For this case, the artifact that emerged from the general design cycle was an academic research project. Thus, the traditional goal for the Conclusion phase of the design cycle for this case is dissemination of the results of the project through published papers. The primary problems encountered in publishing are convincing the members of a research community who have been selected to review the papers sent to a particular venue that the results are (1) interesting, (2) novel, and (3) accessible to the community, that is, well and clearly articulated.

To a great degree, the issue of interest depends on how well directed the research effort was by the patterns *Research Domain Identification, Research Conversation,* and, more generally, *Industry and Practice Awareness.* Research communities as communities of interest by definition have a highly focused awareness. Topics outside the traditional core interests for a research community are frequently rejected as either uninteresting or inappropriate.

Both *Novelty and Significance* in publication are addressed by the pattern of the same name. This pattern suggests ways to increase the salience of a contribution to the research community. The *Aligning with a Paradigm* pattern also makes suggestions on how to make a research presentation appear consonant with the problems found interesting and the techniques found acceptable to a given research community.

Table 5.5 Pattern Application during the Conclusion Phase of Research

Patterns Utilized	Actions Generated
Research Domain Identification (p. 84); Research Conversation (p. 88); Industry/Practice Awareness (p. 116)	These patterns, when successfully applied at earlier phases in the research project design cycle, align the research effort with the terminology and practice of a research community, and make publication of both conference and journal papers easier.
Aligning with a Paradigm (p. 179)	In this phase of the design cycle, this pattern was invoked again to determine exactly which one of several similar paradigms (almost but not quite equated with specific journals) to choose to submit results to.
Style Exemplars (p. 178); Novelty and Significance (p. 181)	These patterns assist in focusing on a specific journal and in making salient in the presentation of research results the novelty and significance of the research. Unless the reviewers perceived both attributes in the research, it will be difficult to publish.
Writing Conference Papers (p. 175); Use of Examples (p. 183)	Application of these patterns assists in successful conference paper preparation.
Writing Journal Papers (p. 176); Use of Examples (p. 183)	Application of these patterns assists in successful journal paper preparation.

At the end of this phase, Buchanan's dissertation (Buchanan, 1991) had been composed and successfully defended, papers based on the dissertation had been accepted by two conferences (Buchanan et al., 1990; Vaishnavi et al., 1993), and a related paper had been accepted by a third conference (Kuechler et al., 1995). The choice of conferences was strongly directed by the "community alignment" patterns mentioned above. All papers made extensive *Use of Examples* to make concrete and more understandable the novel abstraction of smart objects. A fifth publication, a submission to the *Journal IEEE Transactions on Knowledge and Data Engineering* (*TKDE*) was also generated in this phase (Vaishnavi et al., 1997). The choice of journal was made only after much deliberation, guided by the publishing patterns in Chapter 11 of this book, and several "walk-throughs" during which preliminary sketches of a paper were made and evaluated according to the paradigms apparent in a given journal's editorial statement and in exemplar papers published in recent issues of the journal. The ultimate choice of *TKDE* was made when the *Style Exemplars* pattern led to an understanding that the results of the smart object project could be structured very similarly to several published exemplars in that journal. Table 5.5 summarizes all the patterns applied and resulting actions during the Conclusion phase.

This concludes the smart object paradigm use case; however, as elaborated upon in Chapter 2 ("An Example of ICT Design Science Research"), several other research projects based on the smart object paradigm were conducted and resulted in a stream of published work extending over a period of eight-plus years.

Practice, Practice, Practice

While the use of the patterns in this book will assist in solving many of the problems encountered in a design science research effort, patterns are (not) rules and the method we have outlined for their use is simply a guideline from the experience of many design researchers. There is still no other way to fully understand design research than to do it. We suggest that you review "An Example of ICT Design Science Research" in Chapter 2, the textual description of the smart object project, and then, guided by the appropriate patterns and ongoing reference to this chapter — the "how-to" section of this book — plunge into the Awareness of Problem phase for your own design science research project. Good luck!

References

Alexander, C. (1964). *Notes on the Synthesis of Form*. Cambridge, MA, Harvard University Press.

Buchanan, G., Vaishnavi, V., and Nevins, A. (1990). Modeling Operations Management Support Systems. *Proceedings of the IEEE International Symposium on Man, Machine and Cybernetics*, pp. 134–136.

Buchanan, G. (1991). Modeling Operations Management Support Systems. Unpublished doctoral dissertation, Atlanta, GA: College of Business Administration, Georgia State University.

Firebaugh, M.W. (1988). *Artificial Intelligence*. Boston, MA: Boyd & Fraser Publishing Company.

Gladwell, M. (2005). *Blink: The Power of Thinking without Thinking*. New York: Little Brown and Company.

Kuechler, W.L., Lim, N., and Vaishnavi, V.K. (1995). A Smart Object Approach to Hybrid Knowledge Representation and Reasoning Strategies. *Proceedings of the 28th Hawaiian International Conference on Systems Sciences*, pp. 33–41.

Kunda, Z. (1987). Motivated inference: self-serving generation and evaluation of causal theories. *Journal of Personal and Social Psychology*, 53, 669–679.

Murray, R. (2005). *Writing for Academic Journals*. Maidenhead, NY: Open University Press.

Searle, J. (1995). *The Construction of Social Reality*. New York: Free Press.

Vaishnavi, V. Buchanan, G., and Nevins. A. (1993). Smart Objects: A Tool for Building Intelligent Support Systems. *Proceedings of the 26th Hawaiian International Conference on Systems Sciences*, pp. 93–102.

Vaishnavi, V., Buchanan, G., and Kuechler, W. (1997). A Data/Knowledge Paradigm for the Modeling and Design of Operations Support Systems. *IEEE Transactions on Knowledge and Data Engineering*, 9(2), 275–291.

Chapter 6

Creativity Patterns

Creativity

Creativity is an integral part of all intellectual endeavors and is a critical necessity in all areas of research. However, it is a "soft" and poorly understood cognitive skill and is universally acknowledged as difficult or impossible to teach. Fortunately, most individuals are amply creative if only the skill can be focused and directed; directing attention is precisely where patterns excel.

The patterns in this chapter are meta-level patterns and are applicable at any point in a research effort when one faces a problem or situation that needs an inventive solution. In this and subsequent chapters, meta-level patterns are indicated by the superscript M preceding the pattern name. Use the following patterns to harness your creative energies when conducting research:

- MStages of Inventive Process
- MWild Combinations
- MBrain Storming
- MStimulating Creativity

All the above patterns help in using creativity and learning to be creative. *Stages of Inventive Process* describes the stages that one goes through in the inventive process. *Wild Combinations* describes the consideration of combination of solution elements that may not be logically related. *Brain Storming* describes the process of coming up with new ideas or concepts and *Stimulating Creativity* describes the conditions that seem to stimulate creativity.

Sources and References

1. Beveridge, W. (1957). *The Art of Scientific Investigation*, revised edition. Random House.
2. Hadamard, J. (1954). *The Psychology of Invention in the Mathematical Field*. New York: Dover Publications, pp. 1–64.
3. Ladd, G. (1987). *Imagination in Research*, Ames, IA: Iowa State University Press.
4. Wallas, G. (1926). *The Art of Thought*, New York: Harcourt Brace.

ᴹStages of Inventive Process

Intent

Understand and apply the creative (inventive) process.

Context and Applicability

One is at the solution development or some other stage of one's research where conscious logical thinking is not sufficient to make progress. This pattern will assist in tapping into unconscious creative processes.

Description

The inventive process consists of six stages (Hadamard, 1954; Ladd, 1987; Wallas, 1926):

1. Interest
2. Preparation
3. Incubation
4. Illumination
5. Verification
6. Exploitation

Interest: One must have a strong interest in solving the problem if one would like to tap into one's unconscious creative energies. There are two reasons for this. First, one cannot devote the time and energy needed for solving the problem unless one has a strong interest in the problem. Second, one is unlikely to be able to enlist one's unconscious mind in the solution process unless one has a strong interest in the solution of the problem.

Preparation: There is no direct way of communicating with one's unconscious mind. Preparation is a necessary stage for "communicating" the problem to one's unconscious mind and involves the use of all the conscious means that one has available for attempting to solve the problem. Hard work and a degree of physical tiredness and frustration seem to simulate unconscious energies.

Incubation: This is a stage of unconscious mental activity. In this stage, one needs to "sleep over" the problem. One should refrain from consciously thinking over the problem.

Illumination: This is the stage in which the unconscious mind communicates with the conscious mind. Just as the preparation stage is a vehicle for sending messages from the conscious mind to the unconscious mind, the illumination stage involves sending messages from the unconscious mind to the conscious mind. This stage has also been called sudden enlightenment or comprehension (Beveridge, 1957).

Verification: This stage involves conscious voluntary activity just as in the preparation stage. The activities in this stage include the expression of the solution in precise terms and the testing of the validity of the solution offered by the illumination stage using logic and existing knowledge.

Exploitation: This is the last stage in which the work of the previous stages is put to productive use.

Although there is a progression from one stage to the other, as discussed above, the stages do not necessarily follow each other in a strict sequence. One can iterate through one or more of these stages before moving on to the next stage. For example, the verification stage might show the inadequacy of the solution made available by the illumination stage. This serves as preparation for going back to the incubation stage.

Consequences

The practice in the use of this pattern will help one harness one's creative energies in the solution of any problem one might face while conducting research.

Examples

1. Hadamard (1954) describes the use of the inventive process by Henri Poincare, a famous mathematician, in the invention of fuchsian functions. He had found one class of such functions. He knew that these functions constituted only a special case, and his problem was to find the most general form of such functions. He applied persistent conscious effort (preparation stage), which helped him define the problem better, but the solution he was seeking still evaded him. He eventually found the solution unexpectedly while serving in the army.

Sources and References

1. Beveridge, W. (1957). *The Art of Scientific Investigation*, revised edition. Random House.
2. Hadamard, J. (1954). *The Psychology of Invention in the Mathematical Field*. New York: Dover Publications, pp. 1–64.
3. Ladd, G. (1987). *Imagination in Research*. Ames, IA: Iowa State University Press.
4. Wallas, G. (1926). *The Art of Thought*. New York: Harcourt Brace.

ᴹWild Combinations

Intent

Find an unconventional solution to a problem by considering a wild combination of ideas.

Context and Applicability

One is trying to solve a problem or improve an existing solution to a problem. Logical or conventional ideas do not seem to lead to the desired solution. One is now trying to see if the unconventional and wild use of ideas can break the impasse.

Description

1. Combine existing ideas in wild and unconventional ways to produce a large collection of ideas. The trick is to lower one's discriminatory guard so that one can think of novel ways of combining ideas possibly from seemingly unrelated fields.
2. Select the best of these combined ideas. The number of combined ideas can be very large, and it may not be possible to find the more promising of these ideas using conscious logical thinking. The unconscious mind should be tapped to at least find the promising ideas, which then can be analyzed further at the conscious level. An extended experience in the area helps one in developing an aesthetic sense that guides the selection of the promising ideas using the unconscious mind.

Consequences

The use of this pattern can help one move out of the conventional mold and into thinking of novel combinations of ideas for solving a problem.

Examples

1. The invention of the IBM typewriter was the result of thinking in an unconventional way. In a standard typewriter prior to the introduction of the IBM Selectric, the keys were stationary and the paper moved. The (novelty) of the IBM typewriter seems to have been to "let the stationary things move and the moving things be stationary," which was a radical change in the standard typing process. The result was a much faster typewriter.
2. Genetic algorithms are the result of the rather wild combination of the idea of Darwinian evolution with that of mathematical optimization. This has resulted in a novel class of algorithms that can be used in optimizing a function without requiring any knowledge about the nature of the function.
3. Codd (1983) combines the use of relational set theory and predicate logic with that of data modeling to make a bold departure from conventional thinking; also see Chapter 12 (page 209).

Sources and References

1. Codd, E. (1983). A Relational Model of Data for Large Shared Data Banks. *Communications of the ACM,* 13(6), 77–387. Reprinted in *Communications of the ACM, 25th Anniversary Issue*, 26(1), 64–69, January 1983.
2. Hadamard, J. (1954). *The Psychology of Invention in the Mathematical Field*. New York: Dover Publications, pp. 1–64.

ᴹBrain Storming

Intent

Generate a new idea or concept by first generating a large number of ideas, which then are evaluated for their merit.

Context and Applicability

This pattern is more commonly applied by a group of people who collectively would like to generate a novel idea. The premise is that new ideas need to emerge and be nurtured to assess their value before they get killed through our sense of discrimination.

Description

Brainstorming usually is conducted by a group of people. The process is divided into two distinct phases:

1. Generate and record as many ideas as is possible. All ideas and particularly the dumb ideas are very welcome. This is an attempt to tap our unconscious resources to create ideas that would normally get killed before they are born because of our individual or societal sense of "goodness."
2. Evaluate the ideas that have been generated in the first phase for their appropriateness and usefulness.

The separation of the two phases and the deliberate welcoming of "all" ideas is key to the success of the process.

Consequences

The pattern is routinely applied by groups of people in organizational settings to generate new ideas for products. The pattern can also be applied to generate new research ideas by a group of researchers or even by individual researchers.

ᴹStimulating Creativity

Intent

Create conditions for stimulating your creativity, which may otherwise remain dormant.

Context and Applicability

One would like to realize the full potential of using one's creativity in the pursuit of research.

Description

Ladd (1987) lists the following conditions that seem to stimulate unconscious mental processes:

1. *Doubt.* Having or developing a trait for doubting the validity of assumptions that we routinely make and venturing to resolve the doubts is helpful in creating the need for new ideas.
2. *Venturesome attitude.* A degree of research entrepreneurship is needed for a person to delve into the unknown. One must be ready to take risks and not be afraid of mistakes.
3. *Tolerance for uncertainty.* New ideas or insights are often fragmentary and even contradictory. One thus needs to have tolerance for uncertainty to nurture the creation of new ideas.

4. *Diversity.* A creative idea is often a connection between ideas or concepts that were not previously connected. Diversity of interests and experiences is thus helpful to the growth and productive use of the unconscious mind.

5. *Thorough preparation.* Thorough preparation is one of the stages of the inventive process (see *Stages of Inventive Process* pattern). It is, however, not enough to think hard on the problem to fulfill this step in the inventive process. One needs to do whatever one can possibly do consciously to make progress in the solution of the problem. This includes the proper formulation of the problem. One cannot expect a solution from the unconscious mind when the problem is either not formulated at all or is formulated poorly.

6. *Tension.* An intense desire to find a solution is a strong stimulus to the unconscious mind. It is thus helpful to reach a state, a state of tension, where finding a solution is critically important.

7. *Temporary abandonment.* This corresponds to the stage of incubation in the inventive process (see *Stages of Inventive Process* pattern). Developing the habit of consciously abandoning a problem when one is burning to find the solution is thus very important for tapping the unconscious energies. This habit must be learned for becoming creative.

8. *Writing.* Writing is often considered the laborious chore that must be conducted after the fun of invention is finished. The process of writing itself can, however, be a source of new ideas and a way of communicating with the unconscious mind. Writing clarifies ideas and leads to new ideas. It is thus useful also in the creative process.

9. *Exchange with colleagues.* The exchange of ideas with colleagues needs verbalization of ideas. That itself is helpful in the creative process because it leads to the translation of thoughts from the unconscious mind to the consciousness mind.

10. *Freedom from distraction.* It takes effort to "start the engine of the unconscious mind"; and once it has started, one can be in a productive mood. It is thus useful to have stretches of time that are free from other distractions.

11. *Sensitivity to similarities.* The ability to see analogies and to see similarities between seemingly dissimilar things is a tool that can promote the creative association of ideas and concepts. The ability to abstract the differences to see the similarities at a certain level of abstraction is also a useful trait for creativity.

12. *Capturing intuitions.* A productive inventive process needs a two-way flow of messages between the conscious mind and the unconscious mind. Intuitions are the messages that the unconscious mind sends to the conscious mind. These intuitions must be captured as and when they occur. Capturing intuitions and using them also makes one more receptive to the unconscious mind, which promotes more intuitions.

13. *Combinations.* A rich variety of the conditions listed above is stimulating to the unconscious processes. It is thus useful to intersperse writing with temporary abandonment, etc., to provide a rich environment for creative processes.

Consequences

The use and promotion of conditions discussed in this pattern can, over a period of time, improve one's creativity.

Sources and References

1. Ladd, G. (1987). *Imagination in Research*. Ames, IA: Iowa State University Press.

Chapter 7

Problem Selection and Development Patterns

Problem Selection and Development

The patterns in this chapter are applicable to the Awareness of Problem phase of research (see Chapter 2, Figure 2.5): one intends to pursue a design research effort but has not yet identified and developed a research problem on which one can work. The superscript ᴹ preceding the pattern name indicates meta-level patterns.

The patterns in this chapter — *Cost-Benefit Analysis, Being Visionary, Questioning Constraints,* and *Abstraction* — while strongly identified with problem selection and development, are in fact applicable at any point in the research program. The *Research Conversation* pattern is also most naturally found at the problem selection stage of a project, but can also be revisited whenever the research interests of different communities require detailed investigation. The *Solution-Scope Mismatch* and *Complex System Analysis* patterns are also useful in the Suggestion and Development phases of the research. The *Research Domain Identification* pattern is also used in the conclusion phase.

Use the following patterns to help identify and develop a research problem:

- ᴹResearch Domain Identification
- Problem Area Identification
- Problem Formulation
- ᴹResearch Conversation

- Leveraging Expertise
- ᴹCost-Benefit Analysis
- ᴹSolution-Scope Mismatch
- ᴹBeing Visionary
- Research Offshoots
- Bridging Research Communities
- Experimentation and Exploration
- Hierarchical Decomposition
- Interdisciplinary Problem Extrapolation
- ᴹQuestioning Constraints
- Structuring an Ill-Structured Problem
- ᴹAbstraction
- ᴹComplex System Analysis

This chapter guides the reader in using patterns to help in systematically identifying and developing a research problem that best suits the particular circumstances and needs, and that is likely to be pursued successfully.

Research Domain Identification

Intent

Identify a research domain as a starting point for research problem development and for conducting research.

Context and Applicability

One is new to research or intends to start working in a new research domain. The use of this pattern would not be needed if the research domain or topic is suggested naturally by such factors as membership in a highly paradigmatic research community. A research topic can also emerge from reading a research paper or attending a conference; in this case there also would not be any need for the use of this pattern.

Description

One's interest should be the primary criterion for choosing the research domain. This is because high-quality research requires one's full involvement at both the conscious and unconscious levels. It requires the use of one's physical as well as creative energies. A sustained commitment to the research domain is difficult if one does not have an innate interest in the domain.

A close second criterion for choosing the domain should be the availability of resources for conducting the research. The resources that may be needed include access to the relevant literature; research community through conferences, newsletters, etc.; and collaborators, colleagues, or mentors.

One will gain more details on the research domain and a research topic as one progresses further in developing a research problem; these details, in turn, can necessitate a review of the research domain decision. Thus, one should move on to identify the research problem area in the chosen domain if the criteria discussed above have been satisfied, *before* one forms an emotional attachment with the domain or a topic within the domain.

Consequences

A consequence of the use of this pattern is that one will have a good start in the further development of the research problem or a research program. There is greater likelihood that one will enjoy working in the research domain and succeeding in it.

Presentation

How a research domain or topic was chosen by the author is usually not of general interest to the reader of a publication, and thus this information is not included in the presentation of the research.

Example

1. The breadth of the research domain depends on the maturity of the domain. When the domain is relatively new, it can include a large number of topics and issues. As the domain matures, it bifurcates into specialized domains. One test for the existence of a research domain is the existence of a research community with outlets of communication such as conferences, newsletters, special interest groups of professional associations, and journals. There may only be a few such outlets for a young research domain. Examples of current research domains are software metrics, electronic commerce technology, and database systems.

Related Patterns

Problem Area Identification would be the next natural choice of a pattern to use for the further development of a research problem.

Problem Area Identification

Intent

Identify a general set of research questions or problems that are of interest to oneself and to the relevant paradigmatic community.

Context and Applicability

One has identified a research domain in which one wants to conduct research but one does not yet have a research topic. One would like to identify a general set of research questions and issues that are interesting to oneself as well as the research community, and for which adequate resources are potentially available.

Description

Use the following steps along with your creativity (see "Creativity Patterns," Chapter 6) to come up with a set of research problems and issues:

1. Familiarize yourself with the research domain (see *Familiarization with New Area* pattern, page 111).
2. Casually understand the relevant research community (see *Understanding Research Community* pattern, page 112).
3. Use an existing framework to understand the work conducted in the area. If such a framework does not exist, it may be useful to develop at least an informal framework to provide some structure to the literature (see *Framework Development* pattern, page 114).
4. It may be useful to become aware of the state of art in practice and industry (see *Industry and Practice Awareness* pattern, page 116).

Consequences

The pattern will provide a set of research problems and issues that are of interest to the research community or to the practitioner community. The development of a research problem or program should be guided by this set but should not be limited by the set. Interesting research in many cases comes through "stirring the pot" or seeing the research area in new and novel ways.

Problem Formulation

Intent

Identify a specific research problem along with interesting research questions and issues.

Context and Applicability

One has identified a research domain (see *Research Domain Identification* pattern, p. 84). One may have identified a set of problems in the research domain (see *Problem Area Identification* pattern, page 86). Now one wants to find specific research issues that one can work on, identify one's research objectives based on their importance and existing research, and create a problem statement.

Description

Literature search (see *Familiarization with New Area* pattern, page 111) is a major technique in this activity. The identification of goals, the inner environment, and the outer environment (see "Overview of Design Science Research" in Chapter 2) can be useful in understanding the area where the research contribution is needed. Additionally, some understanding of the research community (see *Understanding Research Community* pattern, page 112), the use of or informal creation of a framework (see *Framework Development* pattern, page 114), and an awareness of practice and industry (see *Industry and Practice Awareness* pattern, page 116) is useful in this activity.

The ability to induce valid, focused, and interesting research questions from the information gained from the use of the techniques mentioned above is the most important and useful activity. This requires the use of creativity (see Chapter 6, "Creativity Patterns").

Consequences

The use of this pattern should lead to a research problem that is interesting to an individual and to the research community. How good and significant the research problem and the research questions are depends on how creatively one uses the available information.

Examples

1. The problem is identified based on the observed needs at CERN (Berners-Lee and Cailliau, 1990); also see Chapter 12, page 204. It is clearly stated and scoped.
2. Datta (1998) poses a new research problem; also see Chapter 12, page 196. He therefore justifies the value of the problem to practice as well as the approach used for its solution.
3. The research problem (Purao et al., 2003) is identified from the literature in information systems and software engineering literature and the proposed solution approach is delineated from the prior naïve approaches; also see Chapter 12, page 199.

Sources and References

1. Berners-Lee, T. and Cailliau, R. (1990). WorldWideWeb: Proposal for a Hypertext Project. *http://www.w3.org/Proposal.html.*
2. Datta, A. (1998). Automating the Discovery of AS-IS Business Process Models: Probabilistic and Algorithmic Approaches. *Information Systems Research*, 9(3), 275–301.
3. Purao, S., Storey, V., and Han, T. (2003). Improving Analysis Pattern Reuse in Conceptual Design: Augmenting Automated Processes with Supervised Learning. *Information Systems Research*, 14(3), 269–290.

^MResearch Conversation

Intent

Analyze the literature to find opportunities for research or to "position" the research.

Context and Applicability

One is new to a research area and would like to conduct research that can be published relatively easily. Alternatively, one has a research idea and would like to position it best with respect to the ongoing "research conversations."

Description

1. Identify the research field of relevance and become familiar with the work being conducted in the area using the *Familiarization with New Area* pattern (page 111).

2. Understand the intellectual structure of the research community using the *Understanding Research Community* pattern (page 112).
3. If there is a fairly extensive background in the research area, utilize an existing framework to understand the ongoing research in the area or at least informally develop a framework. The *Framework Development* pattern (page 114) will be useful.
4. Identify the current "puzzles" and research gaps that may be of personal interest.

Consequences

One will become more closely linked to the research community and the current research paradigms being followed by the community. This will help in getting oneself and one's work accepted by the community.

Examples

1. The literature review by Chen (1976) shows the research conversation going on in the data modeling area and the author's attempt to position his research with respect to this conversation; also see Chapter 12, page 207.
2. Using their prior survey work in the field, Choobineh and Lo (2005) were able to identify and join a research conversation on automated database design support systems; see also Chapter 12, page 202.
3. Codd (1970) showed a good understanding of the research in data modeling and positioned his contribution with respect to this research; also see Chapter 12, page 209.
4. Hoare (1978) demonstrated his awareness of the existing research problems in parallel programming and positioned the reported work with respect to these problems; also see Chapter 12, page 214.
5. Denning (1968) provided a good analysis of the existing literature on resource allocation and positioned his contribution in the context of this analysis; also see Chapter 12, page 212.
6. Vaishnavi et al. (1997) used this meta-level pattern in their Publishing stage of the research to identify a journal in which their work could best fit; also see "An Example of ICT Design Science Research" in Chapter 2, "Pattern Usage in the Development of the Smart Object Paradigm" in Chapter 5, and Chapter 12, page 189.
7. The ongoing research conversations in the relevant journals revealed that no algorithm existed for constructing optimal multiway search trees (Vaishnavi et al., 1980); also see Chapter 12, page 216.

Sources and References

1. Chen, P. (1976). The Entity-Relationship Model: Toward a Unified View of Data. *ACM Transactions on Database Systems*, 1(1), 9–37.
2. Choobineh, J. and Lo, A. (2005). CABSYDD: Case-Based System for Database Design. *Journal Management Information Systems*, 21(3), 281–314.
3. Codd, E. (1970). A Relational Model of Data for Large Shared Data Banks. *Communications of the ACM,* 13(6), 377–387. Reprinted in *Communications of the ACM, 25th Anniversary Issue*, 26(1), 64–69, January 1983.
4. Hoare, C. (1978). Communicating Sequential Processes. *Communications of the ACM*, 21(8), 666–677. Reprinted in *Communications of the ACM, 25th Anniversary Issue*, 26(1), 100–106, January 1983.
5. Denning, P. (1968). The Working Set Model for Program Behavior. *Communications of the ACM*, 11(5), 323–333. Reprinted in *Communications of the ACM, 25th Anniversary Issue*, 26(1), 43–48, January 1983.
6. Vaishnavi, V., Buchanan, G., and Kuechler, W. (1997). A Data/Knowledge Paradigm for the Modeling and Design of Operations Support Systems. *IEEE Transactions on Knowledge and Data Engineering*, 9(2), 275–291.
7. Vaishnavi, V., Kriegel, H., and Wood, D. (1980). Optimum Multiway Search Trees. *Acta Informatica*, 14, 119–133.

Leveraging Expertise

Intent

Select a research problem to pursue that can leverage one's strengths and expertise.

Context and Applicability

One has a number of research areas or problems in which one has a general interest. One does not have the time or resources to develop completely new areas of expertise to aid one's research. One would like to choose a research topic that has the best chances of successful completion based on one's current strengths.

Description

One's strengths, expertise, and interest are very important determinants of success for a research project. To leverage one's expertise:

1. Identify the strengths and areas of expertise. Find what areas one is most comfortable in and what areas interest one most. Ask oneself if there is a particular type of experience that provides some unique strength in a certain type of research project.

2. Choose a research topic or project that either utilizes one's unique expertise or strength, or builds on it.

Consequences

Based on this pattern, one will pursue research that utilizes one's current expertise and strength. This is a conservative approach. The downside of this approach is that one will not develop expertise and interest in new research domains.

Examples

1. A person who has worked in the software industry for many years before pursuing research has unique insights into the software development area. This person can bring his or her expertise and strengths to bear on a research project in the software development area as against a research area that does not deal with software development.
2. Choobineh and Lo (2005) leveraged the expertise and insight gained through writing earlier a survey of the area of database design support systems; see also Chapter 12, page 202.
3. Purao et al. (2003) are leveraging their prior research experience in addressing the problem; see also Chapter 12, page 199.

Sources and References

1. Choobineh, J. and Lo, A. (2005). CABSYDD: Case-Based System for Database Design. *Journal of Management Information Systems*, 21(3), 281–314.
2. Purao, S., Storey, V., and Han, T. (2003). Improving Analysis Pattern Reuse in Conceptual Design: Augmenting Automated Processes with Supervised Learning. *Information Systems Research*, 14(3), 269–290.

^MCost-Benefit Analysis

Intent

Use *Cost-Benefit Analysis* to determine if the planned expenditure of resources is justified by the expected research benefits. [Author Note: When an early version of this book was used to teach a class on design science research to graduate students at the Indian Institute of Technology in Delhi, the students expressed surprise that a cost-benefit analysis would be applied to research. We believe this is one of the most important and widely applicable patterns in the book because our experience is that resources, especially time, are always limited. Initial appraisal of the cost-benefit of a research project and reappraisal whenever the project seems "stalled," especially in its early phases, is crucial at many points in a researcher's career. These include finishing a Ph.D. program and, in the United States at least, the pre-tenure (assistant professor) phase of a job at a university.]

Context and Applicability

One is planning to commit to the expenditure of a large amount of resources for a research project. Such resources can be physical equipment such as computers and software, or human resources such as the subjects in an experiment, and time, which is always a scarce resource in any environment, be it business or academic. Determining whether the planned cost justifies the research benefits is required when developing a research proposal for a doctoral degree or a research grant. Most research in industry requires a cost-benefit analysis before committing any resources to the project.

Description

This pattern suggests an analysis of the planned major cost and its expected benefits before one plunges into actual implementation of the plan:

1. Analyze and estimate the expected cost in human and physical resources. Confirm that these resources are available or are likely to be available.
2. Analyze the expected research benefits, that is, the expected research findings and results that can result from the planned expenditure.
3. Explore alternative, less-expensive strategies for carrying out the research. Make a convincing case for the expected benefits outweighing the costs.
4. Develop a detailed plan with milestones so that one can confirm that the expected research benefits are materializing as the project proceeds. Even after starting the project, monitor the costs and benefits. Scale down or even cancel the planned expenditure if the benefits do not justify the further expenditure.

Consequences

This pattern will help explore all the alternatives before one plunges into a strategy for conducting one's research, a strategy that involves a major expenditure in physical or human resources. It will also lead one to analyze the planned cost and see if the expenditure is feasible.

Examples

1. Detailed estimates of human and physical resources were made by Berners-Lee and Cailliau (1990). An attempt was made to reduce the cost of the project without affecting the research benefits; also see Chapter 12, page 204.
2. Vaishnavi et al. (1997) used this meta-level pattern in the Suggestion and Development phases of their research while iterating with different possible solution approaches to their research problem; also see "An Example of ICT Design Science Research" in Chapter 2, "Pattern Usage in the Development of the Smart Object Paradigm" in Chapter 5, and Chapter 12, page 189.

Sources and References

1. Berners-Lee, T. and Cailliau, R. (1990). WorldWideWeb: Proposal for a Hypertext Project. *http://www.w3.org/Proposal.html*.
2. Vaishnavi, V., Buchanan, G., and Kuechler, W. (1997). A Data/Knowledge Paradigm for the Modeling and Design of Operations Support Systems. *IEEE Transactions on Knowledge and Data Engineering*, 9(2), 275–291.

ᴹSolution-Scope Mismatch

Intent

Determine whether an existing solution (or solutions) to a problem can be used when the scope of the problem is expanded or a more complex version of the problem is considered.

Context and Applicability

There exists a good or reasonable solution for a research problem. One can think of a more complex version of the problem or one with expanded scope that is worth solving, one that has either not been addressed thus far in the literature or the available solution is not reasonable. The existing solution technique for the smaller scope problem can be applied to the new problem.

Description

Apply the existing solution technique to the larger problem and analyze the solution. If the solution is acceptable under these conditions, then one has solved the problem using the existing technique. This may be a research contribution if the new problem is important and the application of the solution technique is nontrivial.

If, on the other hand, an analysis of the solution shows that it is not a good solution, then one may have discovered a research problem worth solving. If one can think of a set of such problems with varying complexity, then it is useful to apply the above-cited steps to all these problems. This will provide more information on how the existing solution technique works as the scope of the problem expands. This information will be useful in the exploration of a better solution technique to the set of problems and in making the solution more general.

If there exists more than one solution technique to the limited scope problem that can be applied to the larger scope problem, then the above steps should be applied using all such solution techniques. If the application of any of the existing solution techniques does not lead to a reasonable solution to the more general problem (or problems), then one has made a case for generalizing the existing solution technique (or techniques) or finding a new solution technique. It is better to try generalizing the existing solution technique (or techniques) before trying to come up with a different solution technique.

Consequences

If the application of existing solution technique (or techniques) leads to an acceptable solution for the expanded problem (or problems), then the work may not be as productive as in the case when the solution is less than acceptable. However, in either case, it is a good investment of time. In the former case, one has shown that the existing solution can be extended to the more complex problem and hence there is no need for coming up with a generalized or different solution technique. In the latter case, one has found an interesting research problem that is worth solving.

Examples

1. The limitations of the existing data models to support data independence were demonstrated by Codd (1970); also see Chapter 12, page 209.
2. While analyzing the background literature, Denning (1968) discussed the merits of the Least Recently Used Selection policy for memory management when there is only one process and the weaknesses of the policy when there are many processes; also see Chapter 12, page 212.
3. Vaishnavi et al. (1997) found that a mismatch existed between the available tools and what was needed for constructing and maintaining a support system for complex operations environments; also see "An Example of ICT Design Science Research" in Chapter 2, "Pattern Usage in the Development of the Smart Object Paradigm" in Chapter 5, and Chapter 12, page 189.
4. An efficient algorithm existed for organizing data in the primary storage in optimal fashion (Knuth, 1971) but no such algorithm existed for disk storage (Vaishnavi et al., 1980); also see Chapter 12, page 216.

Related Patterns

■ Easy Solution First (see page 130)

Sources and References

1. Codd, E. (1970). A Relational Model of Data for Large Shared Data Banks. *Communications of the ACM,* 13(6), 377-387. Reprinted in *Communications of the ACM, 25th Anniversary Issue,* 26(1), 64–69, January 1983.
2. Denning, P. (1968). The Working Set Model for Program Behavior. *Communications of the ACM,* 11(5), 323–333. Reprinted in *Communications of the ACM, 25th Anniversary Issue*, 26(1), 43–48, January 1983.
3. Knuth, D. (1971). Optimum Binary Search Trees. *Acta Informatica,* 1, 14–25.
4. Vaishnavi, V., Buchanan, G., and Kuechler, W. (1997). A Data/Knowledge Paradigm for the Modeling and Design of Operations Support Systems. *IEEE Transactions on Knowledge and Data Engineering*, 9(2), 275–291.
5. Vaishnavi, V., Kriegel, H., and Wood, D. (1980). Optimum Multiway Search Trees. *Acta Informatica,* 14, 119–133.

ᴹBeing Visionary

Intent

Envision an improvement in a situation or problem even if the present solution is acceptable.

Context and Applicability

One is familiar with a problem or situation. One is not satisfied with the current solution or situation and can envision an improvement that one thinks is feasible to perform.

Description

Identify the key features, criteria, or attributes of the current situation or the current best solution to a problem. Analyze the current situation and describe the ideal or desired set of features, values for attributes and criteria, and relevant qualitative aspects. That is, create a "vision" for the improvement of the current situation. Critically review the "gap" between the current situation and the desired situation. The analysis need not be exhaustive but should examine if there are any major hurdles in bridging the gap. If the gap seems too large and infeasible to cover, make the gap smaller; that is, revise vision and make it more realistic. One may want to increase the gap once one has gained confidence in covering the smaller gap.

Consequences

The consequences depend on how bold, relevant, valuable, and compelling one's vision is. If the vision is strong, one may become a pioneer in one's field. On the other hand, if the vision is weak, then the result of fulfilling the vision will also be weak. One danger in trying to fulfill a strong vision is that one may not be successful in realizing the vision. Even if one is successful in fulfilling the vision, one will learn much about the problem. Thus, one can hardly lose from being visionary.

Examples

1. Ackoff (1978) in his book published in 1978 listed a number of features that he would like to see in telephone communication systems. Since then, research has made available most of these features (e.g., caller ID).
2. Bentley and Saxe (1979) generalized the perfectly balanced binary search tree into a multidimensional search tree to organize a set of k-vectors (vectors of size k); perfectly balanced binary trees are used for organizing 1-vectors. The performance of the data structure was $\log_2 n \rfloor + k$ for the search operation. This performance is optimal in any comparison-based model. The data structure does not, however, support update (insert and delete) operations efficiently. AVL-trees (Adel'son-Velskij and Landis, 1962), on the other hand, are dynamic versions of the perfectly balanced binary trees. Vaishnavi envisioned whether one could have a dynamic version of the multidimensional search tree proposed by Bentley and Saxe with performance of $O(\log_2 n) + k$. Specifically, it was envisioned that there exists a multidimensional version of the AVL-tree with the desired performance. The vision was fulfilled by Vaishnavi (1984) and later with a number of other similar data structures.
3. Berners-Lee and Cailliau (1990) identified their concerns with how information is accessed and envisioned the concept of "web of information nodes"; also see Chapter 12, page 204.
4. Chen (1976) identified problems with the existing data models and envisioned a solution to the problems; also see Chapter 12, page 207.
5. Codd (1970) revealed his dissatisfaction with the existing data models and envisioned an improvement that would ensure data independence; also see Chapter 12, page 209.
6. Denning (1968) developed a new vision for system resource that moved away from the prevailing approaches of managing the processor and memory resources separately; also see Chapter 12, page 212.

7. Vaishnavi et al. (1997) envisioned the attributes of an ideal operations management support system that needed support; also see "An Example of ICT Design Science Research" in Chapter 2; "Pattern Usage in the Development of the Smart Object Paradigm" in Chapter 5; and Chapter 12 (page 189).

Sources and References

1. Ackoff, A. (1978). *The Art of Problem Solving.* New York: John Wiley & Sons.
2. Adel'son-Velskij, G. and Landis, Y. (1962). An Algorithm for the Organization of Information. *Soviet Mathematik Doklady*, 3, 1259–1263.
3. Bentley, J. and Saxe, J. (1979). Algorithms on Vector Sets. *SIGACT News*, 11(2), 36–39.
4. Berners-Lee, T. and Cailliau, R. (1990). WorldWideWeb: Proposal for a Hypertext Project. http://www.w3.org/Proposal.html.
5. Chen, P. (1976). The Entity-Relationship Model: Toward a Unified View of Data. *ACM Transactions on Database Systems*, 1(1), 9–37.
6. Codd, E. (1970). A Relational Model of Data for Large Shared Data Banks. *Communications of the ACM*, 13(6), 377–387. Reprinted in *Communications of the ACM, 25th Anniversary Issue*, 26(1), 64–69, January 1983.
7. Denning, P. (1968). The Working Set Model for Program Behavior. *Communications of the ACM*, 11(5), 323–333. Reprinted in *Communications of the ACM, 25th Anniversary Issue*, 26(1), 43–48, January 1983.
8. Vaishnavi, V., Buchanan, G., and Kuechler, W. (1997). A Data/Knowledge Paradigm for the Modeling and Design of Operations Support Systems. *IEEE Transactions on Knowledge and Data Engineering*, 9(2), 275–291.
9. Vaishnavi, V. (1984). Multidimensional Height-Balanced Trees. *IEEE Transactions on Computers*, C-33, 334–343.

Research Offshoots

Intent

Find research problems that have resulted from a recent significant research contribution.

Context and Applicability

While examining recent literature in one's research area, one finds a research paper that solves an existing research problem. The research contribution reported in that paper is significant either because the research problem solved is significant or because the approach used in the solution of the problem is significant.

Description

A significant research contribution usually opens up a new research segment. The solution to old problems gives rise to new research problems. Critically review the research paper that solves the existing problem. While examining the paper, try to answer the following questions:

1. Does the paper address all the issues of the problem? Are there issues that still remain unresolved?
2. Has the most general version of the problem been solved?
3. Has the solution to the problem made certain assumptions about the problem? How reasonable are these assumptions? Has the solution weakened or removed certain constraints for the solution of the problem? Are these constraints important?

A positive answer to one or more of the above questions will lead to the identification of a gap in knowledge that needs to be filled.

Consequences

The new research gaps identified are likely to be less significant than the research gap addressed by the research one has examined. This pattern is more useful in identifying relatively small research problems that one can work on rather than a broad stream of research. If the examined research paper has opened up a broad area of research, then there may be scope for identifying a wide area of research that one can work on.

Bridging Research Communities

Intent

Identify a problem that attempts to bridge the gap between two interrelated but distinct research communities.

Context and Applicability

- One wants one's research to have a significant impact and also have a broad audience.
- One has identified two or more research communities that have some overlap in issues that they address.
- One is either familiar with the overlapping research communities or one is willing to learn about these communities and their research. Alternatively,

one can be working on a team where different members of the team have expertise in the knowledge areas of the research communities.

■ The pattern offers significant benefits but there are also pitfalls. Therefore, one needs to use judgment before using this pattern for the identification and development of a research problem. The benefits and pitfalls of the use of this pattern include:

– Benefits:

■ The results of the research will be of interest to a broader audience.

■ There is likelihood of some novelty in the research because of its interdisciplinary nature, which increases its significance.

■ One can also improve the quality of the research by picking and adapting the strong approaches used in the disciplines involved.

– Pitfalls:

■ The involved research communities may use different terminologies and it may be difficult to use a single terminology that satisfies all these communities.

■ There may be a difference in how the overlapping research communities see the research issues and the assumptions that are deemed reasonable.

■ A result of the above two points is that the publication of one's research that bridges the research communities may be difficult or time consuming. This is because it is unlikely for the editor of a research journal to find referees who are well-versed in all the involved disciplines. The editor may choose different referees specializing in the different disciplines. In this case, there is the possibility of the different referees not agreeing on the format or the contents of the reported results.

Description

1. Select two or at most three distinct but interrelated research communities that have distinct approaches or insights to address certain common issues.

2. If not familiar with all the research communities and their literature, then spend time to gain such familiarity. The *Familiarization with New Area* (page 111) or *Understanding Research Community* (page 112) patterns may be useful in this regard. A better solution is to form a team of researchers who have expertise in the research conducted in the research communities. In this case also, some understanding of the research communities by all the members of the team is needed.

3. Identify approaches or insights provided by the research communities for some common problems or issues that have the potential of being combined in a complementary fashion.

Consequences

Application of this pattern should help in identifying an important research project that is of interest to a number of research communities. A successful bridging of the research communities through one's research has the potential for broad impact. Even if one does not execute the research project, the use of this pattern can provide some new insights that one may be able to use in one's research.

Examples

1. The work by Datta (1998) drew heavily from the literature of the research communities of Workflow Management and Business Process Reengineering, as well as grammar discovery as previously applied to software process discovery; also see Chapter 12, page 196.

2. Fraser et al. (1991) used this pattern by developing techniques that enable the use of informal and formal methods together. Specifically, the authors provided a means to make use of the strengths of Structured Analysis in capturing user requirements, and the strengths of Vienna Development Method (VDM) in assuring specification completeness, through a translation mechanism. While the benefits of exploiting the strengths of each community's approach would seem obvious, the authors had to address the comments of the referees, some of which were divergent. Since the publication of this paper, a number of other researchers have pursued the fusing of informal and formal specifications, and tools have been developed that incorporate the fusion.

3. Purao et al.'s (2003) work draws heavily from multiple communities — software engineering, machine learning, human learning, and cognition; also see Chapter 12, page 199.

4. Vaishnavi et al. (1997) bridged the research communities of data modeling, knowledge representation, and software engineering; also see "An Example of ICT Design Science Research" in Chapter 2, "Pattern Usage in the Development of the Smart Object Paradigm" in Chapter 5, and Chapter 12, page 189.

Sources and References

1. Datta, Anindya. (1998). Automating the Discovery of AS-IS Business Process Models: Probabilistic and Algorithmic Approaches. *Information Systems Research*, 9(3), 275–301.

2. Fraser, M., Kuldeep, K., and Vaishnavi, V. (1991). Informal and Formal Requirements Specification Languages: Bridging the Gap. *IEEE Transactions on Systems*, 17, 454–466.

3. Purao, S., Storey, V., and Han, T. (2003). Improving Analysis Pattern Reuse in Conceptual Design: Augmenting Automated Processes with Supervised Learning. *Information Systems Research*, 14(3), 269–290.
4. Vaishnavi, V., Buchanan, G., and Kuechler, W. (1997). A Data/Knowledge Paradigm for the Modeling and Design of Operations Support Systems. *IEEE Transactions on Knowledge and Data Engineering*, 9(2), 275–291.

Experimentation and Exploration

Intent

Explore a new area and the research problems in the area through experimentation.

Context and Applicability

One is working in a research area that is not fully understood. In this area, experiments or prototypes can be built to understand the phenomenon being researched or to test a theory or design principle being developed in the research.

Description

In an area that is not fully understood, experimentation that can proceed through prototyping is an excellent way of gaining familiarity with the area and understanding the real issues that should be addressed. The experimentation reveals complexities of the area and helps in discovering useful areas of investigation. The following steps provide a general guidance for following this approach:

1. If the area has been investigated previously, then form a prototype that incorporates the current knowledge of the area. If the area has not been investigated previously, then build a prototype that incorporates the best hypotheses in the area being investigated.
2. Observe the prototype (experiment) in action and make a systematic record of the performance of the various parameters of interest under varying conditions of execution.
3. Use the knowledge gained through observations to identify the problems and issues that should be researched.

Consequences

One can uncover new areas of research through the use of this pattern. It is also possible that the pattern does not lead to the discovery of completely new or innovative problems of research. In either case, the pattern should increase one's understanding and knowledge of the area, which will help in understanding and isolating the different research issues that are important for the area of research.

Sources and References

1. Tichy, W. (1998). Should Computer Scientists Experiment More? *IEEE Computer*, 31(5), 32–41.

Hierarchical Decomposition

Intent

Hierarchically decompose a research problem to manage the complexity of solving the problem.

Context and Applicability

One has identified a research problem. The problem seems, however, too complex and unlike anything one has seen previously. One may also be unfamiliar with the problem domain.

This pattern assumes that the problem is decomposable. This means that it is possible to decompose the problem into smaller problems such that the solution to the smaller problems can be composed into the solution of the bigger problem. Not all problems are decomposable. An example of a nondecomposable problem would be one in which any solution to one part of a problem can change some aspect of another part of the problem.

Description

Hierarchical decomposition is a standard technique for managing complexity. The guiding steps are as follows:

1. Decompose the problem into sub-parts.
2. Formulate the problem into the problems for solving each of the parts and the problem or combining the solutions for the parts to form the solution for the entire problem.
3. If the parts of the problem are still complex, then repeat the process for each part.
4. Depending on the complexity of the problem, choose one or more parts of the problem at some level of decomposition to be the research problem.

5. If the resources permit, move to a higher-level problem in the hierarchical decomposition after solving the lower-level problems.

Consequences

The technique allows one to concentrate on a relatively smaller problem at one particular time.

Interdisciplinary Problem Extrapolation

Intent

Extrapolate research in one area to create an interesting research problem in a different area.

Context and Applicability

One is familiar with an interesting piece of research in a certain area and thinks that a similar research in a different area would be interesting.

Description

1. Do not confine readings to one's own specialty alone. At the very least, skim through the research in other areas.
2. While skimming through the research in the other areas, ask whether the type of research conducted in the other area would be interesting in one's own area.
3. If the answer to the previous question is positive, then formulate a problem using the benefit of the research conducted in the other area.

Consequences

The pattern can help identify interesting solvable research problems. However, one should be careful in questioning the relevance of the problem and how the problem is formulated to one's own area. If the problem cannot be extrapolated entirely, it may still be possible to adapt the problem or some portion it for one's area of research.

Example

1. Datta (1998) extrapolated the problem of software process discovery to that of discovery of business processes and the use of grammar discovery to reveal process maps; also see Chapter 12, page 196.

Sources and References

1. Datta, A. (1998). Automating the Discovery of AS-IS Business Process Models: Probabilistic and Algorithmic Approaches. *Information Systems Research*, 9(3), 275–301.

ᴹQuestioning Constraints

Intent

Identify a gap in research by questioning constraints that may be explicitly or implicitly imposed on a research problem by the research community.

Context and Applicability

One is starting to work in a new field and thus able to look at the field afresh without being burdened by the prevailing assumptions and constraints. One is aware of some new technology or other developments in the field or related fields that can impact the prevailing constraints used in the current research paradigm being followed in the field.

Description

1. Conduct a quick study of the field to find out the constraints that are part of the current research paradigm being followed in the solution of the research problem.
2. Take a fresh "outside" view of the field to find out whether the constraints are valid. One can also determine the validity of the constraints by technology and other developments that have taken place in the field or related fields. Form a list of constraints that one can argue as being unnecessary.
3. Identify gaps in research by analyzing whether the existing solution to the problem holds when the unnecessary constraints are removed.

Consequences

One will either have a better appreciation of the constraints imposed to the research problem or one will have identified a new research problem (or problems). The identified research problem (or problems) may, however, be too difficult to solve. On the other hand, one may be able to open a new research direction or even a new research paradigm.

Examples

1. There was an implicit constraint in the research community that there is no difference between how data is presented and how it is represented. The work reported by Codd (1970) is largely the result of questioning this constraint; also see Chapter 12, page 209.

Sources and References

1. Codd, E. (1970). A Relational Model of Data for Large Shared Data Banks. *Communications of the ACM*, 13(6), 377–387. Reprinted in *Communications of the ACM, 25th Anniversary Issue*, 26(1), 64–69, January 1983.

Structuring an Ill-Structured Problem

Intent

Provide some structure to an ill-structured problem.

Context and Applicability

One is familiar with a problem usually driven from practice. The problem does not have a clear objective or constraints. There might also be a source of uncertainty in the problem.

Description

1. Identify the key objectives. If there are multiple objectives, prioritize them and drop those objectives that are not as important. Make sure that the objectives being considered are not in conflict with each other.
2. Analyze the nature of objectives. Try to quantify qualitative objectives into quantitative ones.

3. Analyze the constraints for their relevance and drop those constraints that do not seem relevant.
4. Attempt to state the problem in precise formal terms.

Consequences

Some structure and preciseness will be introduced into the problem that originally was ill structured and ill defined. The solution of the problem may still need heuristics or human judgment but it is always better to refine and formalize the problem as much as possible. This opens the possibility of using algorithmic or optimization techniques to parts of the problem, which is preferable to the use of "softer" techniques.

Examples

1. Given the difficulty of automating discovery of complete process descriptions from actual process event traces, Datta (1998) decomposed the total problem into components and demonstrated that a process activity graph (PAG) is an important component of the discovery of AS-IS processes; also see Chapter 12, page 196.
2. Hoare (1978) abstracted the problem of communication between processes and their synchronization to that of finding a simple way for sequential processes to communicate with each other; also see Chapter 12, page 214.
3. The research (Purao et al., 2003) generated a structured approach to the complex problem of expert performance in conceptual design from the machine learning literature; also see Chapter 12, page 199.

Sources and References

1. Datta, A. (1998). Automating the Discovery of AS-IS Business Process Models: Probabilistic and Algorithmic Approaches. *Information Systems Research*, 9(3), 275–301.
2. Hoare, C. (1978). Communicating Sequential Processes. *Communications of the ACM*, 21(8), 666–677. Reprinted in *Communications of the ACM, 25th Anniversary Issue*, 26(1), 100–106, January 1983.
3. Purao, S., Storey, V., and Han, T. (2003). Improving Analysis Pattern Reuse in Conceptual Design: Augmenting Automated Processes with Supervised Learning. *Information Systems Research*, 14(3), 269–290.

^MAbstraction

Intent

Abstract a research problem from its many concrete instances and state the research issues and questions.

Context and Applicability

One is aware of many concrete problems from experience or literature that seem to be somewhat similar. One wants to formulate a deeper research problem from the concrete instances.

Description

1. Use abstraction and creative abilities to think of the underlying issues that give result to the concrete problems.
2. Informally model the underlying phenomenon to see whether the solution of the identified underlying problem will solve the observed concrete problems.
3. Check if the underlying problem can also lead to other concrete problems that one may not have experienced or discovered previously.
4. Define the underlying problem and frame research questions that should be answered to solve the underlying problem.

Consequences

One is able to move from a level of development or ad-hoc problem solution to a research level. One is able to frame research issues and questions that are significant and have a broad impact.

Examples

1. Hoare (1978) abstracts the problem of communication between processes and their synchronization to that of finding a simple way for sequential processes to communicate with each other; also see Chapter 12 (page 214).

Sources and References

1. Hoare, C. (1978). Communicating Sequential Processes. *Communications of the ACM*, 21(8), 666–677. Reprinted in *Communications of the ACM, 25th Anniversary Issue*, 26(1), 100–106, January 1983.
2. Parnas, D. (1998). Successful Software Engineering Research. *Software Engineering Notes*, 23(3), 64–68.

ᴹComplex System Analysis

Intent

Analyze a complex system to find areas where research is needed to improve the performance or effectiveness of the system.

Context and Applicability

One is familiar with or has access to a complex system. One is interested in conducting research that can improve the performance or effectiveness of the complex system.

Description

One should remain alert for deficiencies and problem areas while conducting the following analysis of the complex system:

1. Analyze the static structure of the complex system. Find out what the sub-systems of the system are, as well as how they are related to each other, and apply the same analysis to the subsystems recursively. Most often, one finds that the system is a hierarchical system or a "nearly decomposable system." (The difference between a nearly decomposable system and a hierarchical system is that while the interactions between the subsystems in the former are weak compared to those within the subsystems, such interactions are not negligible.)
2. Analyze the dynamic behavior of the system and study how this behavior is produced.
3. Study the evolution of the system. Complex systems usually are the result of a long process of evolution from a relatively simple system.
4. Attempt a preferably simple representation of the system. The representation of complex systems need not be complex.

Consequences

One will get a deeper understanding of the complex system and how it manages its complexity. One will also be able to see problem areas that can be a starting point for formulating a research problem of relevance to the complex system.

Examples

1. The research problem was identified in the process of analyzing a complex operations environment and its modeling (Vaishnavi et al., 1997); also see "An Example of ICT Design Science Research" in Chapter 2, "Pattern Usage in the Development of the Smart Object Paradigm" in Chapter 5, and Chapter 12, page 189.

Sources and References

1. Simon, H. (1996). *The Sciences of the Artificial*, third edition. Cambridge, MA: MIT Press.
2. Vaishnavi, V., Buchanan, G., and Kuechler, W. (1997). A Data/Knowledge Paradigm for the Modeling and Design of Operations Support Systems. *IEEE Transactions on Knowledge and Data Engineering*, 9(2), 275–291.

Chapter 8

Literature Search Patterns

Literature Search

The patterns in this chapter are applicable to most phases of the research (see Chapter 2, Figure 2.5). One conducts a literature search to understand a research area or to position the research ideas or approaches that one may be considering. The superscript [M] preceding the pattern name indicates meta-level patterns.

The *Industry and Practice Awareness* pattern is most naturally found at the literature search stage of a project, but may also be revisited whenever a detailed investigation of industry techniques in an area may be beneficial — in the Evaluation phase, for example.

Use the following patterns to conduct the literature search:

- Familiarization with New Area
- [M]Understanding Research Community
- Framework Development
- [M]Industry and Practice Awareness

This chapter serves as a guide for using patterns that can help in an effective literature search.

Familiarization with New Area

Intent

Become familiar with a new research area.

Context and Applicability

One is either new to research or working in a different research area. One is exploring working in a new research area. One has identified the domain of research (see *Research Domain Identification* pattern.). One is now interested in becoming familiar with the domain so that one can possibly find a set of research questions or problems that are of interest to oneself and the relevant research community.

Description

Become familiar with the research literature and the research community in the domain by:

- Using Internet resources such as World Wide Web search tools
- Reading literature in the area
- Attending conferences
- Talking to people working in the area
- Casual understanding of a selected research community (see the next pattern, *Understanding Research Community*)

Consequences

One may find oneself unprepared to work in the research area because of inadequate knowledge of the area and the time it will take to acquire that knowledge. The familiarity with the area will also give one a better idea of one's level of interest in the research domain; one may decide not to pursue research in the domain based on this information. If the research community is not highly paradigmatic or if the literature is not well organized, one may find the need to get a deeper understanding of the research community. The use of the *Understanding Research Community* pattern may be needed in such a case. If the literature in the area is extensive and no good published survey is available, then the use of the *Framework Development* pattern may be useful.

Related Patterns

The *Problem Area Identification* pattern can find the current pattern very useful. The current pattern can, in turn, use the *Understanding Research Community* pattern.

ᴹUnderstanding Research Community

Intent

Understand how the community organizes its "intellectual structure" and gain "acceptance" by the community.

Context and Applicability

One is new to the research community. One would like to understand the community. This would help one gain acceptance by the community and become able to influence the community. Understanding the community and one's acceptance by the community would also help report one's research in a way that is acceptable to the editors and reviewers of journals in the community.

Description

1. Use the World Wide Web, conference proceedings, books, and journals to gain knowledge and an understanding of:
   a. The history, foundation, paradigm, and culture of the community
   b. The hot issues, shared beliefs, shared values, and tacit knowledge of the community
   c. The research techniques, procedures, protocols, and tools that the community has accepted as its standard for working on the research issues
   d. The vocabulary used by the community and the level of abstraction and explanation used to communicate research ideas and results
2. Use the understanding gained to know what the intellectual boundaries of the community are. Stay within this boundary unless one wants to enhance the community by extending these boundaries. This is usually an activity for mature researchers.
3. Retain one's individuality and creativeness to pursue issues and research directions that influence and enhance the research community.

Consequences

The use of the pattern can help in one's assimilation into the community. There is, however, a danger that one may get overly assimilated, which can prevent one from offering novel and creative research directions and solutions. Thus, one should try to maintain one's individuality and creativity while using the pattern to gain an understanding of the community and one's acceptance by the community.

Examples

1. Chen's paper (1976) revealed a good understanding of the data modeling research community; also see Chapter 12, page 207.
2. Choobineh and Lo (2005) showed their understanding of the research community gained through earlier survey work; also see Chapter 12, page 202.

3. Denning's paper (1968) showed a good understanding of the research community and its intellectual structure; also see Chapter 12, page 212.

Related Patterns

This pattern is used by the *Problem Area Identification* pattern. Other related patterns include:

- Familiarization with New Area
- Framework Development
- Industry and Practice Awareness
- Aligning with a Paradigm

Sources and References

1. Chen, P. (1976). The Entity-Relationship Model: Toward a Unified View of Data. *ACM Transactions on Database Systems*, 1(1), 9–37, March 1976.
2. Choobineh, J. and Lo, A. (2005). CABSYDD: Case-Based System for Database Design. Journal of Management Information Systems, 21(3), 281–314.
3. Denning, P. (1968). The Working Set Model for Program Behavior. *Communications of the ACM*, 11(5), 323–333. Reprinted in *Communications of the ACM, 25th Anniversary Issue*, 26(1), 43–48, January 1983.

Framework Development

Intent

Develop a framework for a research area that organizes the literature of the area and identifies gaps in knowledge that must be filled.

Context and Applicability

There is fairly extensive knowledge in the research area. However, a good recent survey of the area is not available. One would like to develop a framework of the research conducted in the area. One is interested in doing so to either help write a good survey of the area or to aid in one's research problem.

Description

Use morphological analysis (Zwicky, 1967) to form structures (morphologies) of existing information in the subject area. Use the analysis to derive a classification scheme that can serve as a framework for understanding the existing work in the area as well as for exposing the areas that have not received adequate attention. The development of a good framework is a creative task (see Chapter 6, "Creativity Patterns") but the following steps can serve as a guideline:

1. Collect the entire literature or a good sample of the literature to form the literature base.
2. Analyze key ideas and currently known dimensions and parameters in the literature base.
3. Analyze and abstract this information to form a tentative classification scheme.
4. Populate the classification scheme with the literature in the literature base.
5. Examine the contents of the literature in the different categories of the classification scheme to see if the classification scheme needs revision.
6. Abstract the concepts of the classification scheme to derive its dimensions.
7. Examine and abstract the relationships between the different dimensions to form an initial version of the framework.

Consequences

The pattern should provide a framework for organizing the literature in the research area. A good framework should help in providing new insights into the research domain and identifying important gaps in the existing research. A good framework can be very useful in surveying a research area and can be a contribution by itself.

Examples

1. Chen (1976) described a framework for multilevel views of data and introduced the entity-relationship model using this framework; also see Chapter 12, page 207.
2. The work by Datta (1998) draws from the literature of multiple fields to investigate a problem not currently addressed. The author developed a framework to provide an intellectual structure for the problem addressed; also see Chapter 12, page 196.
3. Purao et al. (2003) positioned their approach through the development of a framework of machine learning techniques; also see Chapter 12, page 199.

Sources and References

1. Chen, P. (1976). The Entity-Relationship Model: Toward a Unified View of Data. *ACM Transactions on Database Systems*, 1(1), 9–37.
2. Datta, A. (1998). Automating the Discovery of AS-IS Business Process Models: Probabilistic and Algorithmic Approaches. *Information Systems Research*, 9(3), 275–301.

3. Purao, S., Storey, V., and Han, T. (2003). Improving Analysis Pattern Reuse in Conceptual Design: Augmenting Automated Processes with Supervised Learning. *Information Systems Research*, 14(3), 269–290.

4. Zwicky, F. (1967). The Morphological Approach to Discovery, Invention, Research, and Construction, in *New Methods of Thought and Procedure*, Zwicky, F. and Wilson, A.G., Eds. New York: Springer-Verlag.

ᴹIndustry and Practice Awareness

Intent

Maintain awareness of the developments in industry and practice.

Context and Applicability

One wants to find research topics that are of relevance and interest to practice and industry. Alternatively, one wants to find applications of one's research to industry.

Description

Use the following strategies to remain abreast of the current practice in industry:

1. Use the same systems and tools as used in the industry. For example, use the programming languages, database systems, design methodologies, and other systems and tools used currently in practice. This will help in experiencing first-hand the problems and issues faced in practice.

2. Read professional and trade magazines to remain aware of the developments in practice.

3. Accept a visiting assignment in an industrial organization of relevance to one's research domain. Participate or observe the actual work being done and abstract the issues and problems arising from this work.

Consequences

To obtain the desired benefits of this pattern, one should be able to identify the problems faced in practice and should be able to abstract them into research problems that are of general interest. That is, one should be careful not to identify oneself too closely with the actual work that one is observing or participating in or with the compromises being taken in carrying out the work.

Examples

1. The research on the World Wide Web (Berners-Lee and Cailliau, 1990) was conducted at CERN and was motivated by problems faced at CERN in linking and accessing information; also see Chapter 12, page 204.
2. Codd (1970) showed a good awareness of the available commercial database management systems and their limitations; also see Chapter 12, page 209.
3. Datta (1998) stressed the real-world aspects of the problem addressed by citing from general nontechnical citations from workflow and process management; also see Chapter 12, page 196.
4. The research (Purao et al., 2003) is motivated by the well-known industry problem of facilitating the reuse of design components; also see Chapter 12, page 199.
5. The research problem (Vaishnavi et al., 1997) was identified by attempting to model real-world operations support systems using Prolog; also see "An Example of ICT Design Science Research" in Chapter 2, "Pattern Usage in the Development of the Smart Object Paradigm" in Chapter 5, and Chapter 12, page 189.

Sources and References

1. Berners-Lee, T. and Cailliau, R. (1990). WorldWideWeb: Proposal for a Hypertext Project. *http://www.w3.org/Proposal.html*.
2. Codd, E. (1970). A Relational Model of Data for Large Shared Data Banks. *Communications of the ACM*, 13(6), 377–387. Reprinted in *Communications of the ACM, 25th Anniversary Issue*, 26(1), 64–69, January 1983.
3. Datta, A. (1998). Automating the Discovery of AS-IS Business Process Models: Probabilistic and Algorithmic Approaches. *Information Systems Research*, 9(3), 275–301.
4. Parnas, D. (1998). Successful Software Engineering Research. *Software Engineering Notes*, 23(3), 64–68.
5. Purao, S., Storey, V., and Han, T. (2003). Improving Analysis Pattern Reuse in Conceptual Design: Augmenting Automated Processes with Supervised Learning. *Information Systems Research*, 14(3), 269–290.
6. Vaishnavi, V., Buchanan, G., and Kuechler, W. (1997). A Data/Knowledge Paradigm for the Modeling and Design of Operations Support Systems. *IEEE Transactions on Knowledge and Data Engineering*, 9(2), 275–291.

Chapter 9

Suggestion and Development Patterns

Suggestion and Development

The patterns in this chapter are applicable to the Suggestion as well as Development phases of research (see Figure 2.5 in Chapter 2). They can assist in determining the strategies that can be employed to develop a solution to a research problem and in generating knowledge that is of general value.

Suggestion and development patterns are normally employed after developing one's research problem to a reasonable level. One would now like to proceed to develop a solution and associated theory. One would like to know the different approaches and techniques that one can use so that one can use them to guide the research.

With reference to Figure 5.2 in Chapter 5, note that the patterns for this chapter are applicable to two phases of the methodology: Suggestion and Development. This is due to the fact that, in practice, iterations between Suggestion and Development occur many times in the course of a typical design science research (DSR) project. Following an initial Suggestion phase, a project proceeds to Development; upon further investigation, the development appropriate to the initial suggestion may well prove impractical or require resources in excess of those available, or may provide information on a new suggestion that is more interesting or more practically implemented. A real-world example of this type of iteration is given in "An Example of ICT Design Science Research" in Chapter 2. The close coupling of the

Suggestion and Development phases have led us to combine the patterns applicable to those phases rather than attempting to separate them according to some arbitrary criteria.

Meta-level patterns in this (and other) chapters are indicated by the superscript ᴹ preceding the pattern name. The patterns in this chapter — *Sketching Solutions, Different Perspectives*, and *Means-Ends Analysis* — while strongly identified with suggestion and development, are in fact applicable at any point in the research program. The patterns *Problem Space Tools and Techniques, Research Community Tools and Techniques, Interdisciplinary Solution Extrapolation*, and *Technological Approach Exemplars* are also most naturally found at the Development stage of a project, but may also be revisited at the Validation stage, when seeking an Evaluation technique for research results that will be acceptable to the research community associated with the target journal.

The following patterns provide guidelines in different aspects of solution and theory development:

- Theory Development
- Approaches for Building Theory
- Hermeneutical and Inductive Approach
- Incremental Theory Development
- ᴹProblem Space Tools and Techniques
- ᴹResearch Community Tools and Techniques
- Empirical Refinement
- Easy Solution First
- Elegant Design
- Divide and Conquer with Balancing
- Hierarchical Design
- Building Blocks
- ᴹSketching Solution
- Emerging Tasks
- Modeling Existing Solutions
- Combining Partial Solutions
- Static and Dynamic Parts
- Simulation and Exploration
- ᴹInterdisciplinary Solution Extrapolation
- ᴹDifferent Perspectives
- General Solution Principle
- Abstracting Concepts
- Using Surrogates
- Using Human Roles
- Integrating Techniques
- ᴹTechnological Approach Exemplars
- ᴹMeans-End Analysis

The first four patterns specifically address the issue of theory generation.

Research is a creative process, and the solution/theory development stage is a particularly creative stage of the research. The patterns listed above can thus only guide researchers in solution and theory development. They cannot by themselves generate the solution and the associated theory.

Theory Development

Intent

Explicitly state the theory that underlies the solution to the research problem.

Context and Applicability

One is interested in explicitly drawing theory from one's research, which can include new ideas and concepts, construction of conceptual frameworks, new methods, models (e.g., mathematical models, simulation models, and data models), in addition to general correlation relationships. In certain fields such as artificial intelligence (AI), the solution (or program) itself can be considered theory. Even in such cases, one would like to explicate the theory from the created artifact and state it formally.

Description

The following patterns provide guidance for constructing theory:

- Approaches to Building Theory (page 122)
- Hermeneutical and Inductive Approach (page 123)
- Incremental Theory Development (page 125)

Consequences

One will become conscious of the theory building aspect of one's research and will get some guidance in an area sometime overlooked in design research.

Example

1. The *smart object paradigm* (Vaishnavi et al., 1997) and its instantiation, the *smart object model*, constitute the theory developed; also see "An Example of ICT Design Science Research" in Chapter 2, "Pattern Usage in the Development of the Smart Object Paradigm" in Chapter 5, and Chapter 12, page 189.

Sources and References

1. Vaishnavi, V., Buchanan, G., and Kuechler, W. (1997). A Data/Knowledge Paradigm for the Modeling and Design of Operations Support Systems. *IEEE Transactions on Knowledge and Data Engineering*, 9(2), 275–291.

Approaches for Building Theory

Intent

Obtain a general understanding of the different approaches for building theory.

Context and Applicability

After identifying and developing the research problem, one would like to identify an approach for building theory while solving the research problem.

Description

Table 9.1 describes four general approaches for developing theory.

Consequences

Based on the research area and the research problem, one can assess the suitability of the approaches suggested by this pattern. It is possible that one may need a combination of these approaches or a completely different approach not suggested by this pattern.

Examples

1. The research reported by Chen (1976) uses the hypothetical and deductive approach to build theory; also see Chapter 12, page 207.
2. The approach used to develop the relational model and its associated theory (Codd, 1970) seems to be hypothetical and deductive; also see Chapter 12, page 209.
3. The research of Vaishnavi et al. (1997) used the hypothetical and deductive approach to build theory; also see "An Example of ICT Design Science Research" in Chapter 2, "Pattern Usage in the Development of the Smart Object Paradigm" in Chapter 5, and Chapter 12, page 189.

Table 9.1 General Approaches for Developing Theory

Hypothetical/ Deductive	*Prototyping (Hermeneutical/ Inductive)*	*Case-Based*	*Historical*
Use intuition, results of past experiments, and literature review to build a solution and associated theory.	Build the solution and the associated theory inductively from prototyping and its documentation without any prior commitment. (Developing the prototype is the experiment.)	1. Build a prototype based on an initial solution and theory. 2. Test the prototype to evaluate the solution. 3. Based on the evidence gathered, revise the solution/ theory and modify the prototype to reflect the revised solution/theory. 4. Iterate through Steps 2 and 3. (Developing the prototype is the experiment.)	Develop solution and theory from previously developed knowledge.

Sources and References

1. Baldwin, D. and Yadav, S. (1995). The Process of Research Investigations in Artificial Intelligence — An Unified View. *IEEE Transactions on Systems*, 25(5), 852–861.
2. Chen, P. (1976). The Entity-Relationship Model: Toward a Unified View of Data. *ACM Transactions on Database Systems*, 1(1), 9–37.
3. Codd, E.F. (1970). A Relational Model of Data for Large Shared Data Banks. *Communication of the ACM*, 13(6), 377–387. Reprinted in *Communications of the ACM, 25th Anniversary Issue*, 26(1), 64–69, January 1983.
4. Vaishnavi, V., Buchanan, G., and Kuechler, W. (1997). A Data/Knowledge Paradigm for the Modeling and Design of Operations Support Systems. *IEEE Transactions on Knowledge and Data Engineering*, 9(2), 275–291.

Hermeneutical and Inductive Approach

Intent

Get a complete understanding of the hermeneutical and inductive approach to building theory.

Context and Applicability

One would like to use the hermeneutical/inductive approach to building theory but is not sure about the details of this approach. One is planning to develop a prototype. One would like to ensure that the theory is developed without bias.

Description

Planning, documentation, data collection, and a conscious effort for removing any bias are key features of this approach:

1. Fully document the design decisions and assumptions. Articulate the reasons behind the decisions and the reasons for rejecting any alternate choices.
2. Separate the roles as prototype builder, observer, and theory builder. Document the design process. Collect data on prototype behavior while varying design features and other parameters of the prototype.
3. To induce a theory:
   a. Write a case-study narrative describing the prototype (experiment) and the data obtained on the prototype behavior.
   b. Seek relationships between prototype design features, parameters, and the results of prototype behavior.
   c. Generalize these relationships.
4. Verify the theory by considering the possibility of alternative theories explaining the data and any contradictory evidence to one's theory.

Consequences

This pattern presents a systematic approach for developing theory. The approach, however, requires considerable effort and time. The conduct of a single research project may only provide an initial set of propositions; the development of theory may require the conduct of many projects possibly using different approaches for theory development (see the *Approaches for Building Theory* pattern, page 122). Alternatively, the use of the *Incremental Theory Development* pattern (page 125) may be more suitable to one's type of research problem.

Sources and References

1. Baldwin, D. and Yadav, S. (1995). The Process of Research Investigations in Artificial Intelligence — A Unified View. *IEEE Transactions on Systems*, 25(5), 852–861.

Incremental Theory Development

Intent

Develop theory in an incremental fashion that addresses the research problem.

Context and Applicability

One's research problem is complex. It is not practical to develop theory at a single point in time. An incremental approach in which theory is developed iteratively and one's problem development and prototype design is carried out to facilitate theory development is more practical.

Description

1. *Frame precise research questions.* Instead of asking how a system that is more capable than an existing system can be built, ask why certain architecture can do what other architectures cannot do. The reformulated question can provide a guide for what should be documented and what kind of data should be collected.
2. *Decide whether you want to validate or invalidate a theory.* The decision will affect the requirements of the prototype that one would like to design.
3. *Construct a theory that addresses the problem.* A theory is a set of propositions that identifies units, states of units, and laws or beliefs about the interaction of units to explain, predict, and describe observations within some boundary. It includes new ideas and concepts, conceptual frameworks, new methods, and models (e.g., mathematical models, simulation models, and data models). Direct the prototype design and development effort to validate or invalidate the theory.
4. *Construct a design based on the theory.* What design flows from the theory? How best can the prototype design validate or invalidate the theory?
5. *Develop a prototype based on the design.* Do not deviate from the chosen design in developing the prototype.
6. *Evaluate the results.* Does the data obtained from exercising the prototype support one's theory and solve the research problem? Keep a log of the results. Both positive and negative evidence in support of the theory is valuable in obtaining a better understanding of the research problem.
7. *Refine the problem, theories, and design based on these results.* If the design and the resulting prototype validate the theory, then one has achieved one's objective. Otherwise, the work already done will have provided a better understanding of the implications of the theory and its true applicability to the research problem. Use this improved understanding to revise the problem, theory, and design to correct the deficiencies.

Consequences

This use of this pattern will help in iteratively improving one's understanding of the research problem and in generating a theory that best addresses the problem. Depending on the state of the art in the problem domain, an understanding of why an artifact does not work as expected can be valuable research information.

Example

1. Choobineh and Lo (2005) augment the prior approaches with the case-based approach to the design of the prototype to further incremental development of the theory; also see Chapter 12, page 202.

Sources and References

1. Baldwin, D. and Yadav, S. (1995). The Process of Research Investigations in Artificial Intelligence — An Unified View. *IEEE Transactions on Systems*, 25(5), 852–861.
2. Choobineh, J. and Lo, A. (2005). CABSYDD: Case-Based System for Database Design. *Journal of Management Information Systems*, 21(3), 281–314.

ᴹProblem Space Tools and Techniques

Intent

Identify tools and techniques applicable to the problem space.

Context and Applicability

One has identified and developed a research problem. One would like to evaluate the problem space for the tools and techniques that can be used to obtain new knowledge in the context of the research questions. One would like to be guided by the nature of the phenomenon and the research questions rather than the traditions of the relevant research community.

Description

1. Study the nature of the phenomenon relevant to the research questions.
2. Utilize one's general knowledge of research tools and techniques to see what tools and techniques must be used to obtain knowledge relevant to the research questions.

3. See if there is a promising tool or technique that has been overlooked by the research community.
4. Revisit the Problem Identification and Development phase to see if the research problem should be refocused to better utilize the identified tools and techniques.

Consequences

One will choose tools and techniques that one thinks are appropriate to the solution of the research problem without being directly influenced by the traditions of the relevant research community. In case the research field is new, the pattern will provide opportunity for the use of applicable techniques that have not been used thus far.

Examples

1. The research reported by Chen (1976) departs from the prevailing research culture and uses graphics for data modeling; also see Chapter 12, page 207.
2. Machine learning techniques are used to instantiate theories of expert cognition in conceptual design (Purao et al., 2003); also see Chapter 12, page 199.

Sources and References

1. Chen, P. (1976). The Entity-Relationship Model: Toward a Unified View of Data. *ACM Transactions on Database Systems*, 1(1), 9–37.
2. Purao, S., Storey, V., and Han, T. (2003). Improving Analysis Pattern Reuse in Conceptual Design: Augmenting Automated Processes with Supervised Learning. *Information Systems Research*, 14(3), 269–290.

ᴹResearch Community Tools and Techniques

Intent

Identify the tools and techniques that the relevant research community uses for solving problems similar to one's own research problem.

Context and Applicability

One has developed a research problem. One may have independently identified research tools and techniques based on the nature of the problem (see the *Problem*

Space Tools and Techniques pattern, page 126). One would like to identify the tools and techniques commonly used by the relevant research community for solving similar problems so that one's research benefits from past work.

Description

1. Use literature search (and the corresponding patterns) to find similar problems in the literature.
2. Find out the tools and techniques that have been used in such problems and assess their effectiveness through the knowledge that has been generated by the use of these techniques.

Consequences

One will gain knowledge about the research tools and techniques that have been used by other researchers for solving similar problems. This will help in making an informed decision for choosing tools and techniques for solving one's research problem.

Examples

1. Berners-Lee and Cailliau (1990) proposed to use prototyping as the vehicle for conducting research; prototyping is commonly used for conducting similar types of research; also see Chapter 12, page 204.
2. Choobineh and Lo (2005) used the commonly used research techniques in the field — prototype building followed by experimentation; also see Chapter 12, page 202.
3. Vaishnavi et al. (1997) built their solutions on top of existing models and concepts; also see "An Example of ICT Design Science Research" in Chapter 2, "Pattern Usage in the Development of the Smart Object Paradigm" in Chapter 5, and Chapter 12, page 189.

Sources and References

1. Berners-Lee, T. and Cailliau, R. (1990). WorldWideWeb: Proposal for a Hypertext Project. *http://www.w3.org/Proposal.html*.
2. Choobineh, J. and Lo, A. (2005). CABSYDD: Case-Based System for Database Design. *Journal of Management Information Systems*, 21(3), 281–314.
3. Vaishnavi, V., Buchanan, G., and Kuechler, W. (1997). A Data/Knowledge Paradigm for the Modeling and Design of Operations Support Systems. *IEEE Transactions on Knowledge and Data Engineering*, 9(2), 275–291.

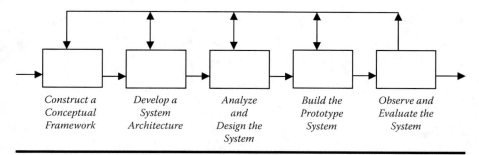

Figure 9.1   Stages of empirical refinement.

Empirical Refinement

Intent

Develop a solution to the research problem through iterations of system development, empirical observation, and refinement.

Context and Applicability

The use of system development as a research process is appropriate to the research problem. The research involves designing a complex system in an area where either no theory exists or only fragments of theory are available to guide the design.

Description

1. Based on the current state of knowledge in the area, construct a conceptual framework, develop a system architecture, analyze and design a system based on the architecture, and build a prototype system based on the design (see Figure 9.1).

   Follow the following steps iteratively until an acceptable solution and an understanding of the underlying phenomenon is reached:

2. Observe the behavior of the constructed system under realistic conditions. Collect data that documents the behavior, deficiencies, and other interesting attributes.
3. Use the data collected in Step 2 to get a better understanding of the underlying phenomena and issues. Use this understanding to improve the conceptual framework and system architecture to remove the deficiencies. Redesign the system and modify the prototype to reflect the new architecture and conceptual framework.

Consequences

One will get a better understanding of the problem domain and appropriate solutions. One may still not have a fully developed theory but one will be able to develop better systems, and a theory will emerge over time.

Examples

1. The research conducted in designing the first time-sharing operating system reflects this pattern. There was little understanding of how such a system should be designed and what demands would be placed on it by its users. Starting with an initial rudimentary design that had severe deficiencies, the design was improved through successive cycles of empirical observation and design until an acceptable system was developed. The successive building process itself helped in building a theory.
2. Research in artificial intelligence has generally followed the strategy suggested by this pattern. For example, the progress in developing an acceptable theorem-proving system was the result of iterative searching for heuristics and refining the system using the new heuristics.
3. Plans for future work in (Berners-Lee and Cailliau, 1990) indicated plans for refinement and empirical observation; also see Chapter 12, page 204.
4. Empirical observation and refinement are planned for the future work of (Purao et al., 2003); also see Chapter 12, page 199.

Sources and Reference

1. Berners-Lee, T. and Cailliau, R. (1990). WorldWideWeb: Proposal for a Hypertext Project. *http://www.w3.org/Proposal.html*.
2. Nunamaker, J., Chen, M., and Purdin, T. (1991). Systems Development in Information Systems Research. *Journal of Management Information Systems*, 7(3), 89–106.
3. Purao, S., Storey, V., and Han, T. (2003). Improving Analysis Pattern Reuse in Conceptual Design: Augmenting Automated Processes with Supervised Learning. *Information Systems Research*, 14(3), 269–290.
4. Simon, H. (1996). *Sciences of the Artificial*, third edition. Cambridge, MA: MIT Press.

Easy Solution First

Intent

Try an easy solution first.

Context and Applicability

One has a research problem for which there seems to exist a relatively simple solution. One is not sure whether the simple solution will constitute a significant contribution.

Description

Good research never attempts to make the simple complex. One should therefore not even try to make the solution complex, or make it look complex when there seems to be a simple solution to the research problem.

In many cases, the seemingly simple solutions turn out to be rather complex or do not turn out to be appropriate solutions for the problem. Trying the simpler solution first will help determine at a small cost the complexity of the problem and its appropriateness for further research efforts.

1. If there seems to be a simple solution to the research problem, use the solution to solve the problem and evaluate the solution.
2. If the simple solution works and provides a reasonable solution, then one need not pursue the problem any further. Depending on the importance of the problem and whether the solution is nontrivial, the solution may be worth reporting as a research note or paper. The solution will also deepen one's understanding of the problem area and help one in coming up with new research questions that may be worth pursuing.
3. If the solution does not work or leads to a solution that is not reasonable, then one has a better foundation for trying a reasonable solution for the problem. At this point, one can utilize one's familiarity with the easy solution to see if it can be applied or extended in a certain way for the solution of the problem. If this approach does not work, then one needs to try a different solution technique.

Consequences

The use of this pattern will provide enhanced confidence that one has not tried to come up with a complex solution while there existed an equally good simple solution for the problem. This information also will help one in motivating the solution at the time of reporting the research.

Examples

1. To provide a proof of concept, the project proposal (Berners-Lee and Cailliau, 1990) attempts a simple solution instead of an elegant solution that would be more complex; also see Chapter 12, page 204.

2. Fraser and Vaishnavi (1997) addressed the problem of having a model that can be used to assess the maturity of a software development organization in incorporating formal specifications in its development process. There already existed a well-known model for measuring the general maturity of an organization called the Capability Maturity Model (CMM) (Paulk et al., 1995). The model was, however, more general than the one the authors were seeking. An organization could be at a high maturity level for incorporating formal specifications but at a lower maturity level according to CMM.

A relatively simple approach to the problem was to adapt the already-known maturity model, CMM, to maturity in using formal specifications. Rather than coming up with a new maturity measurement model, the authors tried the simple approach first. Using the simple approach, the authors came up with a model that essentially projected CMM to the use of formal specifications. The resulting model was interesting but not significant by itself. The authors, however, built upon the simple model to construct a stronger model that suggests strategies for moving to a higher maturity level.

Sources and References

1. Berners-Lee, T. and Cailliau, R. (1990). WorldWideWeb: Proposal for a Hypertext Project. *http://www.w3.org/Proposal.html*.
2. Fraser, M. and Vaishnavi, V. (1997). A Formal Specification Maturity Model. *Communication of the ACM*, 40(1), 95–103.
3. Paulk, M., Weber, C., Curtis, B., and Chrissis, M. (1995). *Capability Maturity Model: Guidelines for Improving the Software Process*. Reading, MA: Addison-Wesley.

Elegant Design

Intent

Design an artifact that is general and can be described functionally.

Context and Applicability

The research involves creating an artifact, that is, something that does not exist in nature but must be created. One would like to construct a general design, one that can be completely described in functional terms, that is, the properties of the artifact in terms of what it does rather than the details of the construction and organization of the artifact.

Description

First, cast the design problem in the framework of the *Sciences of the Artificial* artifact (Simon, 1996); see "Overview of Design Science Research" in Chapter 2. View the artifact or the intended artifact as an interface between a given inner environment and an outer environment while meeting a set of desired goals.

The ideal generality of the artifact is achieved when the artifact is independent of the outer environment; that is, the artifact will function even when the outer environment is changed.

The ideal in descriptive simplicity is achieved when one can describe or predict the behavior of the artifact without having to describe how the artifact is constructed or organized using the inner environment.

Ideally, one would like the artifact to be independent of both the outer and inner environments. This would mean that the way the artifact is designed is such that one does not have to describe its inner or outer environment. Although the ideal may not be achieved, it would be good to let the artifact approximate this ideal. This would constitute ideal design.

Consequences

The pattern provides useful insights into generality and simplicity, which make the design of an artifact elegant even if the ideals set by the pattern are not fully realized. Complete external and inner environment independence is an ideal but the principle is a useful metric for evaluating the elegance of possible designs.

Examples

1. The proposed system (Berners-Lee and Cailliau, 1990) is general and is described functionally; also see Chapter 12, page 204.
2. The relational data model (Codd, 1970) is a general model that can be functionally described; also see Chapter 12, page 209.
3. The working set model (Denning, 1968) is an elegant model that is general and can be described simply; it can be described in terms of its properties; also see Chapter 12, page 212.
4. Hoare (1978) proposed a rich language for parallel processing, CSP, that is both simple and general; also see Chapter 12, page 214.
5. The principle of data hiding (Parnas, 1998) makes the design of a software module independent of the internal changes in the design of another module, X, on which it depends. This, in turn, makes the design more general — the module implementation of X can be changed without affecting the design of the module. The principle also improves the descriptive simplicity of the

module because the module must be described in terms of what it does rather than its implementation.

6. Consider the design of a watch (Simon, 1996). A poorly designed watch would only keep accurate time if it was not moved; a better design would work regardless of movement, but fail if it became wet; and an even better design would work perfectly even if one went scuba diving with it.

One can describe a watch by simply saying that it keeps time; one does not have to describe the parts of the clock and how they are organized to say what the clock does. The design of the clock does not depend to a large extent on the exact material that is used for building the clock.

A poorly designed clock would require the user to unscrew the back and manually adjust springs and gears. A better design would only require the user to routinely wind the clock; and an even better design would require nothing of the user at all — the clock would simply tell accurate time.

7. A system modeled using the smart object paradigm (Vaishnavi et al., 1997) has the characteristics of an elegant design, as does its instantiation, the smart object model itself; also see "An Example of ICT Design Science Research" in Chapter 2, "Pattern Usage in the Development of the Smart Object Paradigm" in Chapter 5, and Chapter 12, page 189.

Sources and References

1. Berners-Lee, T. and Cailliau, R. (1990). WorldWideWeb: Proposal for a Hypertext Project. *http://www.w3.org/Proposal.html*.
2. Codd, E.F. (1970). A Relational Model of Data for Large Shared Data Banks. *Communication of the ACM*, 13(6), 377–387. Reprinted in *Communications of the ACM, 25th Anniversary Issue*, 26(1), 64–69, January 1983.
3. Denning, P. (1968). The Working Set Model for Program Behavior. *Communications of the ACM*, 11(5), 323–333. Reprinted in *Communications of the ACM, 25th Anniversary Issue*, 26(1), 43–48, January 1983.
4. Hoare, C. (1978). Communicating Sequential Processes. *Communications of the ACM*, 21(8), 666–677. Reprinted in *Communications of the ACM, 25th Anniversary Issue*, 26(1), 100–106, January 1983.
5. Parnas, D. (1998). Successful Software Engineering Research. *Software Engineering Notes*, 23(3), 64–68.
6. Simon, H. (1996). *Sciences of the Artificial*, third edition, Cambridge, MA: MIT Press.
7. Vaishnavi, V., Buchanan, G., and Kuechler, W. (1997). A Data/Knowledge Paradigm for the Modeling and Design of Operations Support Systems. *IEEE Transactions on Knowledge and Data Engineering*, 9(2), 275–291.

Divide and Conquer with Balancing

Intent

Manage complexity by dividing the problem into identical smaller problems.

Context and Applicability

One is trying to solve a complex research problem. The problem can be divided into a set of similarly sized, smaller problems. The solutions of the smaller-sized problems can be combined into the solution of the original problem.

Description

1. Divide the problem into identical but smaller problems of equal or nearly equal size. Preferably, the number of such smaller-sized problems should be two.
2. Examine the smaller problems and see if they can be solved.
3. If the smaller problems are solvable, then combine the solution of the smaller-sized problems with the solution for the original problem.
4. If the smaller problems are still complex, then recursively apply Steps 1 through 3 to get the solution for each of the problems and then combine these solutions to form the solution for the original problem.

Consequences

The technique, if applicable, is an excellent technique for managing complexity.

Example

1. The pattern has been used with success in the design of a large number of efficient algorithms and data structures. Examples of such algorithms and data structures include the binary search algorithm, dynamic data and file structures such as B-trees, and efficient data structures for multidimensional and spatial data such as k-d trees and quad trees (Samet, 1989).

Sources and References

1. Samet, H. (1989). *The Design and Analysis of Spatial Data Structures*. Reading, MA: Addison-Wesley.
2. Simon, H. (1996). The *Sciences of the Artificial*, third edition. Cambridge, MA: MIT Press.

Hierarchical Design

Intent

Design a complex system using the divide and conquer strategy.

Context and Applicability

The research involves designing a complex system. The system is nearly decomposable, which means that the system can be decomposed into subsystems such that the interactions *between* subsystems are weaker than the interactions *within* subsystems.

Description

This pattern designs a system by designing its subsystems and the interactions between the subsystems. By properly designing the subsystems and the interactions between them, one creates an artifact that satisfies the desired purpose.

Follow the following steps in designing the system:

1. Divide the system into subsystems (each subsystem should be significantly smaller than the original system).
2. For each subsystem, explore if there is an existing design that can be used. If there exists such a design, then use the design.
3. If any subsystem can be designed without further decomposition, then design it; otherwise, use the procedure recursively for designing the subsystem.
4. Design the interactions between the subsystems such that the overall system meets the desired objectives.

Use the following guidelines for decomposing a system into its subsystems in the above procedure:

- Reduce the number of interconnections and interactions between the subsystems.
- Reduce the dependency between subsystems. Subsystem A may require input from subsystem B, but ideally it should be capable of operating to at least some degree even if subsystem B fails.

Consequences

Applying this pattern will produce a design that consists of a hierarchical arrangement of subsystems, with each subsystem being reasonably independent of the others. The main advantage of using this pattern is a significant reduction in the complexity of designing the system.

Examples

1. The overall proposed system (Berners-Lee and Cailliau, 1990) is based on the design of a browser and a server, and interaction between the two; also see Chapter 12, page 204.

2. Consider a system that consists of ten subsystems, each of which interacts with all the other subsystems (Simon, 1996). There are a total of 45 interactions between subsystems. Overall, a total of 55 items (10 systems and 45 interactions) must be designed. Next, consider a system that consists of 100 subsystems, each of which interacts with all the other subsystems. In this case, there are 4950 interactions to design, which means that a total of 5050 systems and interactions must be designed. This means that a system that has 10 times as many subsystems is nearly 100 times as complex! The cause of this rapidly growing complexity is the growth in the number of interactions as the number of subsystems increases.

    The solution to the growth in complexity is to reduce the number of interactions by designing hierarchically. By dividing the system into subsystems, each of which consists of a relatively small number of subsystems, the number of interactions is reduced.

    There are several advantages to this approach. The system is simpler because the number of connections is dramatically reduced. The system is easier to understand because we can understand it in "chunks" of ten items at a time, rather than having to understand all 100 parts at once. The system is easier to modify because we can often change the design of a single subsystem without necessarily impacting the other subsystems. In addition, the system is easier to debug because we can diagnose "hierarchically" — checking each subsystem rather than each individual part.

3. Vaishnavi et al. (1997) designed the smart object paradigm in a hierarchical manner, separating its logical and architectural views, and separating the paradigm from its instantiation; also see "An Example of ICT Design Science Research" in Chapter 2, "Pattern Usage in the Development of the Smart Object Paradigm" in Chapter 5, and Chapter 12, page 189.

Related Pattern

Divide and Conquer with Balancing (page 135) pattern differs from the current pattern in that it is not limited to design and it divides the problem into *identical* smaller problems.

Sources and References

1. Berners-Lee, T. and Cailliau, R. (1990). WorldWideWeb: Proposal for a Hypertext Project. *http://www.w3.org/Proposal.html*.
2. Simon, H. (1996). *The Sciences of the Artificial*, third edition. Cambridge, MA: MIT Press.
3. Vaishnavi, V., Buchanan, G., and Kuechler, W. (1997). A Data/Knowledge Paradigm for the Modeling and Design of Operations Support Systems. *IEEE Transactions on Knowledge and Data Engineering*, 9(2), 275–291.

Building Blocks

Intent

Divide the given complex research problem into smaller problems that can form the building blocks for solving the original problem.

Context and Applicability

The problem is large or complex. It is difficult to fully understand or solve the entire problem. The problem can, however, be decomposed into smaller problems that are less complex.

Description

1. Decompose the problem into smaller problems — building blocks.
2. Continue decomposing each of the resulting problems until they are understandable and amenable to finding a solution.
3. Solve each of the problems at the lowest level of decomposition.
4. Recursively assemble the solution to smaller problems to find the solution to the parent problems until the original problem is solved.

Consequences

The pattern, if applicable, is very useful for managing complexity and error. It is easier to test the correctness of a solution of a building block than that of the entire problem. It is also relatively simple to modify or change the solution to a simple building block.

Related Patterns

Hierarchical Design (page 136). The current pattern is similar to the *Hierarchical Design* pattern, which, however, focuses on designing a complex system.

Sources and References

1. Simon, H. (1996). *The Sciences of the Artificial,* third edition. Cambridge, MA: MIT Press.

ᴹSketching Solution

Intent

Sketch a solution to the given research problem (or the design of a complex system).

Context and Applicability

There is danger in overlooking or not giving enough priority to the solution of a critical component of the solution. If the solution to the critical component cannot be found, then any effort invested in solving the other components would be wasted.

Description

1. Sketch a solution of the problem involving the use of building blocks or subsystems and their respective solutions.
2. Verify that the entire problem can be solved if the solution to the identified building blocks is found. Check if there is any missing building block.
3. Identify the critical components (building blocks) whose solution is either critical to the solution of the entire problem or which seem to be difficult problems to solve. Use this information to prioritize the problem components that need to be solved first.

Consequence

This pattern complements the *Building Blocks* and *Hierarchical Design* patterns. Its use ensures that one's efforts are directed at solving the right sub-problems and in the right order to be most productive in the solution of the complete problem.

Example

1. Berners-Lee and Cailliau (1990) provide an outline of their solution in the proposal; also see Chapter 12, page 204.

Related Patterns

- Building Blocks (page 138)
- Hierarchical Design (page 136)

Sources and References

1. Berners-Lee, T. and Cailliau, R. (1990). WorldWideWeb: Proposal for a Hypertext Project. *http://www.w3.org/Proposal.html*.
2. Simon, H. (1996). *The Sciences of the Artificial*, third edition. Cambridge, MA: MIT Press.

Emerging Tasks

Intent

Identify the next task that can contribute to the solution of the research problem and let the succeeding tasks emerge.

Context and Applicability

The research problem is large or complex. It is not possible to break up the problem into sub-problems; see *Hierarchical Design* pattern (page 136) and *Building Blocks* pattern (page 138). One may not be able to find all the tasks that can contribute to the solution of the problem but one may be able to find the first such task.

Description

This pattern uses an incremental and iterative approach along with creativity (see Chapter 6, "Creativity Patterns") for the solution of the problem:

1. Instead of thinking about the solution to the entire problem, think about finding a task that can contribute to the solution of the problem.
2. While conducting the first task, see if one or more tasks emerge as the next task. Start working on this task. (While engaged in performing the first task, one may be unconsciously engaged in finding the next task that can help

solve the problem. Moreover, performance of the first task will provide previously unavailable information to assist in a more complete analysis.)
3. Continue this process until the complete solution is found.

Consequences

This pattern helps in a situation where one is overwhelmed by the complexity or difficulty of the research problem. It allows the use of an incremental approach for the solution of the problem and the use of creativity. The work in finding a task, especially the first task, serves as a vehicle for the "preparation" stage of the creative process (see the pattern, *Stages of Inventive Process*, page 76). The progress in finding the complete solution may be slow but it will be continuous.

Modeling Existing Solutions

Intent

Model existing solutions to similar problems to develop a solution approach.

Context and Applicability

One would like to find the best approach to the solution of the problem based on the existing solutions for similar problems.

Description

1. Identify problems that are "similar" to one's own research problem. This requires the ability to see analogies and to abstract problems and solutions.
2. Learn the solution approaches, concepts, and principles used for solving the similar problems.
3. Apply the gained knowledge to the solution of the problem. This may require modifying or adapting the solution possibly using other research patterns.

Consequences

This pattern lets one learn from other problems and their solutions. This can provide useful insights and even a useful solution approach. The risk in using this pattern is that it may hinder the finding of a unique approach that is not used for the solution of other similar problems.

Example

1. Vaishnavi et al. (1980) used the existing solution for the problem for binary search trees as a basis for the solution of the corresponding problem for multi-way search trees; also see Chapter 12, page 216.

Sources and References

1. Kuhn, T. (1996). *The Structure of Scientific Revolutions*, third edition. Chicago: The University of Chicago Press.
2. Simon, H. (1996). *The Sciences of the Artificial*, third edition. Cambridge, MA: MIT Press.
3. Vaishnavi, V., Kriegel, H., and Wood, D. (1980). Optimum Multiway Search Trees. *Acta Informatica*, 14, 119–133.

Combining Partial Solutions

Intent

Find and combine partial solutions to parts of the research problem to form the entire solution.

Context and Applicability

One cannot find a similar problem for which a solution exists that one can possibly adopt or modify for the solution. There may, however, exist partial solutions that may be relevant to some part of the problem.

Description

1. Identify existing solutions that satisfy some of the requirements for the solution of your problem.
2. Select those solutions that are best suited to the problem.
3. Extract concepts and ideas from the chosen solutions that seem to be promising for the solution of the problem.
4. Based on the "mined" concepts and ideas, form a tentative solution for the problem.
5. Modify and refine the solution to best suit the problem.

Consequences

The pattern is useful when other techniques for developing a solution do not work. The pattern may be difficult to use because it requires the ability to "mine" ideas from a number of existing solutions and putting them to use in innovative ways.

Examples

1. The proposed project (Berners-Lee and Cailliau, 1990) builds on the use of hypertext and HTML; also see Chapter 12, page 204.
2. In solving the problem addressed by Datta (1998), the author drew heavily from the work done on using grammar discovery as a means to software process discovery; also see Chapter 12, page 196.
3. Vaishnavi et al. (1997) brought together concepts from semantic data modeling, rule-based inferencing models, and object-oriented design models into the smart object model; also see "An Example of ICT Design Science Research" in Chapter 2, "Pattern Usage in the Development of the Smart Object Paradigm" in Chapter 5, and Chapter 12, page 189.

Sources and References

1. Berners-Lee, T. and Cailliau, R. (1990). WorldWideWeb: Proposal for a Hypertext Project. *http://www.w3.org/Proposal.html.*
2. Datta, Anindya. (1998). Automating the Discovery of AS-IS Business Process Models: Probabilistic and Algorithmic Approaches. *Information Systems Research*, 9(3), 275–301.
3. Vaishnavi, V., Buchanan, G., and Kuechler, W. (1997). A Data/Knowledge Paradigm for the Modeling and Design of Operations Support Systems. *IEEE Transactions on Knowledge and Data Engineering*, 9(2), 275–291.

Static and Dynamic Parts

Intent

Separate the static and dynamic parts of the research problem and solve them separately.

Context and Applicability

One is trying to solve a research problem that has time-dependent components. To manage the complexity of the problem, one would like to separate the static parts of the problem from its dynamic parts. It should be possible to separate the static and dynamic portions of the problem.

Description

1. Separate the static and dynamic components of the problem.
2. Find separate basic solutions for the static and dynamic portions of the problem.
3. Combine the two types of solution in an innovative manner to form a seamless overall solution.

Consequences

The pattern lets one concentrate on the static and dynamic portions of the problem separately. The dynamic portion of the problem may be more difficult and may need greater attention. The pattern helps in doing so by separating the static and dynamic issues.

Simulation and Exploration

Intent

Understand and predict the behavior of a designed system.

Context and Applicability

One has designed a system or would like to explore alternative designs for the system. The system and its design are complex such that one cannot fully understand or predict the behavior of the system without actually implementing the design and building the system. The actual building of the system is, however, infeasible or cumbersome. One would like to understand or predict the behavior of the designed system without having to build the system.

Description

Simulation (Navidi, 2006) is a way of imitating the "inner" and the "outer environments" (Simon, 1996) in the small, implementing the design using the imitated inner and outer environments, and observing the behavior of the imitated system to understand and predict the behavior of the actual system. Digital computers and simulation languages have greatly facilitated simulation. Use the following steps to conduct simulation:

1. Identify or create objects (parts) that imitate the objects used in the real-life system.
2. Use the design to organize the parts into a system that imitates the desired system. The organization must not violate any organization principles of the inner environment of the real-life system.
3. Subject the imitated system to a range of environments that imitate the outer environment of the real-life system.
4. Observe the behavior of the imitated system to understand or predict the behavior of the real-life system.

Consequences

This pattern will provide new knowledge under the following two situations:

1. One fully understands the inner environment but one does not fully understand or cannot analyze the system behavioral implications of the known organization principles used in the design.
2. The natural laws governing the inner environment are not fully known. However, abstract properties and laws governing the inner environment are known. The simulation helps in understanding or predicting abstract behavioral properties of the real-life system. Even in the first situation, the understanding of the inner environment and the prediction of behavior are at a certain level of abstraction.

Examples

1. One has designed a motor vehicle. It is not possible to fully understand or predict the behavior of the vehicle under varying driving conditions. One simulates the motor vehicle to understand and predict the behavior of the vehicle under a variety of driving conditions that mimic actual driving conditions.
2. One wants to design the layout of a bank in terms of the number of tellers, dimensions of the bank, etc. One simulates the layout using different abstract components that mimic actual components relevant to the design. One implements the simulation on a computer and observes the lengths of lines that will be formed in front of the tellers using a variety of distribution patterns for the arrival of customers.

Sources and References

1. Navidi, W. (2006). *Statistics for Engineers and Scientists.* Boston, MA: McGraw-Hill
2. Simon, H. (1996). *The Sciences of the Artificial,* third edition. Cambridge, MA: MIT Press.

ᴹInterdisciplinary Solution Extrapolation

Intent

Explore the possibility that a solution or solution approach to a problem in one discipline or domain can be applied in or adapted to a different domain.

Context and Applicability

One is aware of a significant solution or a solution approach to a problem or a class of problems in a domain different from that of one's own research problem. One has a hunch that there is some similarity between the problems in the two domains. (Virtually all successful researchers admit to following hunches.)

Description

1. Critically examine the problem in the other domain for which there exists a significant solution.
2. Abstract the problem in the other domain and one's own research problem to see if there is any relationship between the two problems at the conceptual level. The relationship may not be obvious and one may need to use some creative abilities to see the relationship (see Chapter 6, "Creativity Patterns").
3. If one finds a relationship, attempt to translate or adapt the solution in the other domain to provide a solution to the research problem.

Consequences

The application of this pattern can lead to an obvious solution to the problem. On the other hand, clever translation of knowledge in one domain to a different domain can lead to significant new insights and solutions.

Examples

1. The smart object paradigm (Vaishnavi et al., 1997) fuses together concepts from databases, software engineering, artificial intelligence, and operating systems; also see "An Example of ICT Design Science Research" in Chapter 2, "Pattern Usage in the Development of the Smart Object Paradigm" in Chapter 5, and Chapter 12, page 189.
2. The research reported by Datta (1998) developed its solution using published work in multiple fields — process modeling, workflow management, computer science (finite-state machines); also see Chapter 12, page 196.
3. Purao et al. (2003) extrapolated the use of machine learning techniques from their traditional use in fields such as information retrieval to the reuse of conceptual design; also see Chapter 12, page 199.

Sources and References

1. Datta, Anindya. (1998). Automating the Discovery of AS-IS Business Process Models: Probabilistic and Algorithmic Approaches. *Information Systems Research*, 9(3), 275–301.
2. Purao, S., Storey, V., and Han, T. (2003). Improving Analysis Pattern Reuse in Conceptual Design: Augmenting Automated Processes with Supervised Learning. *Information Systems Research*, 14(3), 269–290.
3. Vaishnavi, V., Buchanan, G., and Kuechler, W. (1997). A Data/Knowledge Paradigm for the Modeling and Design of Operations Support Systems. *IEEE Transactions on Knowledge and Data Engineering*, 9(2), 275–291.

ᴹDifferent Perspectives

Intent

Look at the research problem from different perspectives.

Context and Applicability

There is no obvious approach to the solution of the research problem. One would like to look at the problem in a new way to help find a solution.

Description

Look at the problem from different and unorthodox ways. For example, if the research question is how to make a system more reliable, ask how to prevent it from being unreliable or less reliable. This may require the use of one's creativity (see Chapter 6, "Creativity Patterns"). By looking at a problem from a novel perspective, an interesting solution may emerge for the problem.

Consequences

This pattern can lead to a novel solution when "using the beaten track" approaches do not work or do not lead to good solutions.

Examples

1. Chen (1976) used the framework presented in his paper to provide a new perspective on data modeling; also see Chapter 12, page 207.
2. Codd (1970) provided a new perspective on data modeling by raising it to a higher level of abstraction; also see Chapter 12, page 209.
3. Denning (1968) provided two new perspectives on the research problem: initiating the development of analytical models for program behavior and the use of a unified approach for process scheduling and core memory management; also see Chapter 12, page 212.
4. Vaishnavi et al. (1997) used this pattern to come up with a novel general solution; also see "An Example of ICT Design Science Research" in Chapter 2, "Pattern Usage in the Development of the Smart Object Paradigm" in Chapter 5, and Chapter 12, page 189.

Sources and References

1. Chen, P. (1976). The Entity-Relationship Model: Toward a Unified View of Data. *ACM Transactions on Database Systems*, 1(1), 9–37.
2. Codd, E.F. (1970). A Relational Model of Data for Large Shared Data Banks. *Communication of the ACM*, 13(6), 377–387. Reprinted in *Communications of the ACM, 25th Anniversary Issue*, 26(1), 64–69, January, 1983.
3. Denning, P. (1968). The Working Set Model for Program Behavior. *Communications of the ACM*, 11(5), 323–333. Reprinted in *Communications of the ACM, 25th Anniversary Issue*, 26(1), 43–48, January 1983.

General Solution Principle

Intent

Construct a general solution for a class of problems.

Context and Applicability

One is trying to develop a general solution for solving a class of problems. One can find a general concept that is common to all the problems in the class.

Description

1. Find a general concept or principle that explains and unifies the class of problems.
2. Find a general problem-solving technique that is appropriate to the problems in the class.
3. Integrate the general concept or principle identified in Step 1 into the problem-solving technique, resulting in a general technique for solving the class of problems.
4. Use the generalized technique to develop a general solution for the class of problems.
5. Tune the general technique to specific problems in the class of problems to take advantage of special restrictions or constraints.

Consequences

The use of this pattern can lead to interesting and useful solutions to entire classes of problems. The use of the technique, however, may be difficult, as it requires conceptualizing general concepts and principles behind a class of problems and then integrating these concepts into a general solution technique. Dynamic programming technique is particularly amenable to this integration of concepts through its optimality principle.

Examples

1. Chen (1976) showed that the entity-relationship model generalizes the prevailing data models, the network model, the relational model, and the entity-set model; also see Chapter 12, page 207.
2. Denning (1968) developed the working set model as a general model for program behavior that can be used for processor and memory allocation as well as for balancing processor and memory demands; also see Chapter 12, page 212.
3. CSP (Hoare, 1978) can be used to represent solutions for a number of problems related to communication and synchronization of processes; also see Chapter 12, page 214.

4. The proposed prototype design (Purao et al., 2003) is general in that it can be used in multiple modes; also see Chapter 12, page 199.
5. Vaishnavi et al. (1997) presented a general solution for a class of problems — supporting complex operations environments — that can be instantiated to particular solutions; also see "An Example of ICT Design Science Research" in Chapter 2, "Pattern Usage in the Development of the Smart Object Paradigm" in Chapter 5, and Chapter 12, page 189.
6. Starting with an instance of the research problem for multiway search trees, Vaishnavi et al. (1980) developed a general solution principle for a class of problems; also see Chapter 12, page 216.

Sources and References

1. Chen, P. (1976). The Entity-Relationship Model: Toward a Unified View of Data. *ACM Transactions on Database Systems*, 1(1), 9–37.
2. Denning, P. (1968). The Working Set Model for Program Behavior. *Communications of the ACM*, 11(5), 323–333. Reprinted in *Communications of the ACM, 25th Anniversary Issue*, 26(1), 43–48, January 1983.
3. Hoare, C. (1978). Communicating Sequential Processes. *Communications of the ACM*, 21(8), 666–677. Reprinted in *Communications of the ACM, 25th Anniversary Issue*, 26(1), 100–106, January 1983.
4. Purao, S., Storey, V., and Han, T. (2003). Improving Analysis Pattern Reuse in Conceptual Design: Augmenting Automated Processes with Supervised Learning. *Information Systems Research*, 14(3), 269–290.
5. Vaishnavi, V., Buchanan, G., and Kuechler, W. (1997). A Data/Knowledge Paradigm for the Modeling and Design of Operations Support Systems. *IEEE Transactions on Knowledge and Data Engineering*, 9(2), 275–291.
6. Vaishnavi, V., Kriegel, H., and Wood, D. (1980). Optimum Multiway Search Trees. *Acta Informatica*, 14, 119–133.

Abstracting Concepts

Intent

Abstract concepts from existing solutions to generalize the solutions and to theorize.

Context and Applicability

Solutions to specific instances or special cases of the research problem are available in the literature. One would like to abstract these solutions to form a general solution that will have wider applicability and impact.

Description

Use creativity (see Chapter 6, "Creativity Patterns") and the following steps as a guide to develop abstract concepts from existing solutions to specific instances of a general problem to develop a solution to the general problem:

1. Analyze and understand the solutions to the special cases of the general problem and the underlying concepts behind these solutions.
2. Generalize the underlying concepts to more abstract but simple general concepts that encompass the underlying concepts in existing solutions.
3. Test the general concepts for their applicability to the solution of the special cases of the general problem. The resulting solution should be as good as the original solutions to the special cases of the general problem. If the solution does not cover all the special cases or does not lead to solutions that are comparable to original existing solutions, then modify the abstractions and or the level of abstraction.
4. Use the abstract concepts to develop a solution to the general problem.

Consequences

The pattern lets one capitalize on previous work and learn from it to develop a solution to a general problem. The pattern contributes to theory by developing general concepts and other constructs that have general applicability. If successfully applied, the pattern can lead to contributions that have a broad impact.

Examples

1. The research by Datta (1998) developed its solution by abstracting the prior work on software process modeling via grammar discovery; also see Chapter 12, page 196.
2. Vaishnavi et al. (1997) used this pattern to derive the broad specifications of the smart object paradigm; see also "An Example of ICT Design Science Research" in Chapter 2, "Pattern Usage in the Development of the Smart Object Paradigm" in Chapter 5, and Chapter 12, page 189.

Sources and References

1. Datta, Anindya. (1998). Automating the Discovery of AS-IS Business Process Models: Probabilistic and Algorithmic Approaches. *Information Systems Research*, 9(3), 275–301.

2. Vaishnavi, V., Buchanan, G., and Kuechler, W. (1997). A Data/Knowledge Paradigm for the Modeling and Design of Operations Support Systems. *IEEE Transactions on Knowledge and Data Engineering*, 9(2), 275–291.

Using Surrogates

Intent

Use surrogates to aid research.

Context and Applicability

One is trying to establish a result for something that is either abstract or something that is difficult or costly to work with directly. One would like to explore the use of a surrogate for the subject of the result. Examples of surrogates include Structured Analysis (surrogate for an informal requirements specification language), students in a graduate programming class (surrogate for programmers), a commercial software package (surrogate for a component of a research prototype), etc.

Description

1. Analyze the nature of the subject for which one is considering to use a surrogate.
2. Analyze the essential requirements of the subject to serve the intended research purpose.
3. See if the subject or some component of the subject can be substituted by a surrogate that is easier to handle or obtain. Make sure that the surrogate does not violate any research assumptions.
4. Use the surrogate in the research instead of the actual subject.

Consequences

If a suitable surrogate is found, the research may benefit in terms of time, effort, or cost. Finding a suitable surrogate, however, may be difficult. Additional care must be taken to make sure that the use of the surrogate does not bias the research results.

Example

1. Fraser et al. (1991) used Structured Analysis as a surrogate for an informal requirements specifications language and VDM (Vienna Development Method) as a surrogate for a formal requirements specification language.

Sources and References

1. Fraser, M., Kumar, K., and Vaishnavi, V. (1991). Informal and Formal Requirements Specification Languages: Bridging the Gap. *IEEE Transactions on Systems*, 17, 454–466.

Using Human Roles

Intent

Use human roles for ideas and concepts.

Context and Applicability

The research is attempting to develop concepts, methods, etc. to automate an activity that is currently performed by human beings. One would like to study and utilize human roles for performing the activity to get ideas and inspiration.

Description

1. Clearly define the activity that the research is targeting to automate.
2. Identify a task activity and a human role for performing the activity that closely resembles the activity of interest to the research.
3. Closely observe the performance of the activity by one or more human beings (subjects). Use audiovisual methods to record the performance of the activity, along with verbal protocols that the subjects may provide.
4. Analyze the observations and protocols.
5. Use the analysis to aid in the development of concepts, models, and methods that can be used to automate the activity.

Consequences

The use of the pattern can provide useful insights and ideas that can be used to develop the desired solution.

Example

1. Vaishnavi et al. (1997) studied human supervisory tasks in nuclear power plants to formulate them for automation through meta-level rules; also see "An Example of ICT Design Science Research" in Chapter 2, "Pattern Usage in the Development of the Smart Object Paradigm" in Chapter 5, and Chapter 12, page 189.

Sources and References

1. Vaishnavi, V., Buchanan, G., and Kuechler, W. (1997). A Data/Knowledge Paradigm for the Modeling and Design of Operations Support Systems. *IEEE Transactions on Knowledge and Data Engineering*, 9(2), 275–291.

Integrating Techniques

Intent

Integrate existing techniques, models, or solutions in areas of their respective strengths.

Context and Applicability

One is working on a research problem for which there exists no single technique that can provide a desirable solution. However, there exist multiple techniques that have nonoverlapping strengths and weaknesses in their use for solving the problem.

Description

1. Analyze the strengths and weaknesses of each of the techniques in relation to the requirements for the solution of the problem.
2. Design an informal framework (see *Framework* Development pattern, page 114) that can incorporate the available techniques in the solution of the problem in such a manner that the techniques are used in only those areas where they have strengths for the solution of the problem.
3. Check to see that all aspects of the problem are covered. Fill in any gaps in the solution of the problem.
4. Think of ways to integrate the techniques in the solution of the problem. This may require the creation of new constructs or concepts (see Chapter 6, "Creativity Patterns").
5. Think of ways to make the integrated technique conceptually simple and elegant without sacrificing its effectiveness for the solution of the problem.

Consequences

The use of this pattern can lead to useful and significant techniques, models, or solutions. In certain cases, the contribution can cross discipline or paradigm boundaries, which is good for the advancement of knowledge but can also make it more difficult to communicate the results.

Examples

1. Work from multiple fields — process modeling, workflow management, computer science — was synthesized by Datta (1998) to provide three novel approaches to real-world process discovery; also see Chapter 12, page 196.
2. CSP (Hoare, 1978) abstracted and integrated a number of ideas for expressing parallel computations; also see Chapter 12, page 214.
3. The Smart Object paradigm (Vaishnavi et al., 1997) integrates techniques from data modeling, knowledge representation, and object modeling areas; also see "An Example of ICT Design Science Research" in Chapter 2, "Pattern Usage in the Development of the Smart Object Paradigm" in Chapter 5, and Chapter 12, page 189.

Sources and References

1. Datta, Anindya. (1998). Automating the Discovery of AS-IS Business Process Models: Probabilistic and Algorithmic Approaches. *Information Systems Research*, 9(3), 275–301.
2. Hoare, C. (1978). Communicating Sequential Processes. *Communications of the ACM*, 21(8), 666–677. Reprinted in *Communications of the ACM, 25th Anniversary Issue*, 26(1), 100–106, January 1983.
3. Vaishnavi, V., Buchanan, G., and Kuechler, W. (1997). A Data/Knowledge Paradigm for the Modeling and Design of Operations Support Systems. *IEEE Transactions on Knowledge and Data Engineering*, 9(2), 275–291.

ᴹTechnological Approach Exemplars

Intent

Use known exemplars to aid solution development.

Context and Applicability

One has general ideas on how the research problem can be solved but is not sure how these ideas can be operationalized. There exist exemplars in the literature that show how others have solved similar types of problems.

Description

Exemplars are low-level paradigms (or patterns) that can be used for the solution of the problem. Here are some steps to serve as a guideline:

1. Find papers that can generally serve as exemplars for the solution of your research problem.
2. Select one or more papers that closely relate to the problem and seem to be influential.
3. Analyze the selected papers to mine a paradigm or pattern that one can use for conducting the research.
4. Instantiate the paradigm in terms of the research problem and its requirements.

Consequences

The pattern can help the researcher in gaining tacit and operational knowledge for the conduct of research. It can also serve as a "safe" method for producing knowledge that will be accepted by a paradigmatic research community relatively easily. The disadvantage of the use of the pattern is that it reinforces conformity and may not encourage the conduct of a research in a novel or unorthodox manner.

Example

1. Vaishnavi et al. (1997) used this meta-level pattern in the Evaluation phase of their research to decide what validation techniques they should use in their research; also see "An Example of ICT Design Science Research" in Chapter 2, "Pattern Usage in the Development of the Smart Object Paradigm" in Chapter 5, and Chapter 12, page 189.

Sources and References

1. Kuhn, T. (1996). *The Structure of Scientific Revolutions*, third edition. Chicago: The University of Chicago Press.
2. Vaishnavi, V., Buchanan, G., and Kuechler, W. (1997). A Data/Knowledge Paradigm for the Modeling and Design of Operations Support Systems. *IEEE Transactions on Knowledge and Data Engineering*, 9(2), 275–291.

ᴹMeans-Ends Analysis

Intent

Use means-ends analysis to reach a desired solution state.

Context and Applicability

One knows what the desired solution state of the research problem is but does not know how to reach this state.

Description

This pattern prescribes a process that successively finds the means for narrowing the gap between the end and start states:

1. Precisely describe the desired solution state (end state) and the problem state (start state). Analyze the difference between the two states.
2. Look for methods that can be employed in narrowing the difference between the two states.
3. Employ the most promising method and observe the state that has resulted using the method. If the gap between end state and the resulting state has narrowed, then the use of the method has been successful. Otherwise, use an alternative method.
4. If there still is a gap between end state and the state resulting from the use of the method, then treat the state as the new start state and repeat Steps 2 through 4. Otherwise, one has found a solution to the problem.

Consequences

The advantage of the use of the pattern is that it lets one focus on the goal that the research should achieve. This makes one's research focused and spurs one's creativity (see Chapter 6, "Creativity Patterns"). The disadvantage is that at some point in the process, one may reach a blind alley; at that point one may not know of a method that reduces the gap between the end and start states. It may also lead one to a solution that is not direct or elegant.

Example

1. Vaishnavi et al. (1997) used this meta-level pattern along with the *Sketching Solution* pattern in developing their solution to their research problem; also see "An Example of ICT Design Science Research" in Chapter 2, "Pattern Usage in the Development of the Smart Object Paradigm" in Chapter 5, and Chapter 12, page 189.

Sources and References

1. Simon, H. (1996). *The Sciences of the Artificial*, third edition. Cambridge, MA: MIT Press.
2. Vaishnavi, V., Buchanan, G., and Kuechler, W. (1997). A Data/Knowledge Paradigm for the Modeling and Design of Operations Support Systems. *IEEE Transactions on Knowledge and Data Engineering*, 9(2), 275–291.

Chapter 10

Evaluation and Validation Patterns

Evaluation and Validation

The patterns in this chapter are applicable to the Evaluation phase of the research (see Figure 2.5 in Chapter 2). One has developed a solution that one thinks is correct and one has a hypothesized a number of claims about one's solution. Now one would like to evaluate and validate that solution and the claims about the solution that will be acceptable to the research community.

The following patterns provide vehicles for the evaluation and validation of the developed solution:

- Demonstration
- Experimentation
- Simulation
- Using Metrics
- Benchmarking
- Logical Reasoning
- Mathematical Proofs

These patterns vary in terms of their appropriateness and the strength with which they can establish the validity of a solution. The *Demonstration* pattern provides the weakest form of validation. It may, however, be appropriate if the solution is novel and solves a problem for which no solution exists. On the other extreme, the

Mathematical Proofs pattern provides the strongest form of validation. The strength of the *Logical Reasoning* pattern depends on the strength and preciseness of its arguments and assumptions. It is generally an alternative or supplement to the use of *Experimentation* and *Simulation* patterns. *Experimentation* and *Simulation* patterns are useful when the problem is complex and not amenable to a mathematical proof. The use of the *Using Metrics* pattern is valuable in *Experimentation*, *Simulation*, and *Mathematical Proofs* patterns. It helps in quantifying the claims about the solution. The *Benchmarking* pattern is a weaker form of the *Using Metrics* pattern and is useful along with the *Experimentation* and *Simulation* patterns; it is used when suitable metrics are not available.

The use of one or more of the above listed patterns can help in convincing oneself and the research community of the validity and value of the solution. This, in turn, is very important in publishing one's results.

Demonstration

Intent

Demonstrate that the solution is realizable and valid in predefined situations.

Context and Applicability

One has developed a situation for a problem. The problem or the solution is such that it is not possible to mathematically prove the correctness of the solution. One would still like to demonstrate that the solution is realizable and works for a set of predefined situations. The pattern is particularly relevant when demonstration of a solution itself would be considered a contribution.

Description

1. Construct the solution. This may mean the construction of a prototype for the solution. The construction of the solution will show that the solution is realizable.
2. Demonstrate that the constructed solution is reasonable for a set of predefined situations. These situations should be predefined and not created to suit the solution. They should be constructed to exercise the problem variations.

Consequences

The demonstration of the solution may show the inadequacies of the solution. On the other hand, it may show that the solution is feasible and acceptable. Exhaustive testing of the solution will increase confidence in the solution. If the test situations are designed properly, then the construction of the solution and its testing for these situations can demonstrate the validity of the solution.

Examples

1. Berners-Lee and Cailliau (1990) proposed to demonstrate the solution through a prototype; also see Chapter 12, page 204.
2. Chen (1976) demonstrated the use of the entity-relationship model for database design and the use of the proposed diagrammatic technique with the use of an example; also see Chapter 12, page 207.
3. The developed system (Choobineh and Lo, 2005) was validated through an expert evaluation of a demonstration of the system for two expert designers; also see Chapter 12, page 202.
4. Codd (1970) demonstrated the various attributes of the new model through an example; also see Chapter 12, page 209.
5. Datta (1998) provided a walk-through of a simple case to show the merits of the process activity graphs (PAGs) relative to the metrics used; also see Chapter 12, page 196.
6. Hoare (1978) showed the versatility of CSP using the language for expressing the solutions to many classical programming problems; also see Chapter 12, page 214.
7. Purao et al. (2003) demonstrated the proposed solution through the construction and exercise of a prototype; also see Chapter 12, page 199.
8. Vaishnavi et al. (1997) used demonstration through examples and cases as a vehicle for evaluation; also see "An Example of ICT Design Science Research" in Chapter 2, "Pattern Usage in the Development of the Smart Object Paradigm" in Chapter 5, and Chapter 12, page 189.

Sources and References

1. Berners-Lee, T. and Cailliau, R. (1990). WorldWideWeb: Proposal for a Hypertext Project. http://www.w3.org/Proposal.html.
2. Chen, P. (1976). The Entity-Relationship Model: Toward a Unified View of Data. *ACM Transactions on Database Systems*, 1(1), 9–37.
3. Choobineh, J. and Lo, A. (2005). CABSYDD: Case-Based System for Database Design. *Journal of Management Information Systems*, 21(3), 281–314.
4. Codd, E.F. (1970). A Relational Model of Data for Large Shared Data Banks. *Communications of the ACM*, 13(6), 377–387. Reprinted in *Communications of the ACM, 25th Anniversary Issue*, 26(1), 64–69, January 1983.
5. Datta, A. (1998). Automating the Discovery of AS-IS Business Process Models: Probabilistic and Algorithmic Approaches. *Information Systems Research*, 9(3), 275–301.

6. Hoare, C. (1978). Communicating Sequential Processes. *Communications of the ACM*, 21(8), 666–677. Reprinted in *Communications of the ACM, 25th Anniversary Issue,* 26(1), 100–106, January 1983.

7. Purao, S., Storey, V., and Han, T. (2003). Improving Analysis Pattern Reuse in Conceptual Design: Augmenting Automated Processes with Supervised Learning. *Information Systems Research,* 14(3), 269–290.

8. Vaishnavi, V., Buchanan, G., and Kuechler, W. (1997). A Data/Knowledge Paradigm for the Modeling and Design of Operations Support Systems. *IEEE Transactions on Knowledge and Data Engineering,* 9(2), 275–291.

Experimentation

Intent

Use experimentation to validate or reject a set of hypotheses associated with the claims about the solution.

Context and Applicability

One has developed a set of hypotheses related to the claims about the solution (usually a system). One cannot prove these hypotheses mathematically or logically. One needs to generate data from the system and then use this data to validate or reject one's hypotheses.

Description

The nature of experiment and the validation of hypotheses depend on the type of experiment. These types, in turn, depend on the approach used in developing the solution. Table 10.1 outlines the different types of experiments and the corresponding method of hypotheses testing.

The hypothetical/deductive experimentation involves constructing a prototype for the sole purpose of testing a set of hypotheses. There is, however, a danger of some bias in the creation of the prototype. It may not be possible to completely eliminate the bias and thus stating the bias that may affect the results is important. One should, however, try to minimize the bias using such strategies as separating the prototype creation and testing, using different environments for prototype creation and testing, defining the tests before constructing the prototype, and using an available system if possible.

In general, an experiment must satisfy the following criteria that have a bearing on the confidence or generality of the results established by the experiment:

Table 10.1 Experiment Types and Corresponding Method of Hypotheses Testing

Hypothetical/ Deductive	Prototyping (Hermeneutical/ Inductive)	Case-Based	Historical
Use intuition, results of past experiments, and a literature review to build the system with the intent of testing a set of hypotheses. Testing the system under varying environments is the experiment. *Collect the experimental data and analyze it to accept or reject the hypotheses.*	Build the system and the associated hypotheses inductively from prototyping and its documentation without any prior commitment. Developing the system is the experiment. *Analyze the prototyping documentation to qualitatively accept or reject the hypotheses.*	Build a prototype based on an initial set of hypotheses. As the prototyping progresses, one will get a deeper knowledge of the problem. Use this knowledge to modify the hypotheses and the prototype guided by the revised hypotheses. Developing the prototype is the experiment. *Use documentary evidence from the prototype to accept or reject the hypotheses.*	Develop a solution and hypotheses from previously developed systems. Observing past systems is the experiment. *Accept or reject hypotheses based on cumulative data from past systems.*

- *Construct validity:* the surrogates for constructs that cannot be readily observed in the experiment must be valid substitutes.
- *Internal validity:* the experiment must not involve constructs that influence the observed behavior other than those that are part of the hypotheses.
- *External validity:* if the results of the experiment are supposed to be general but are tested in a simulated limited environment, one should be able to argue that the results are generalizable.
- *Reliability:* the experiment should be replicable.

Consequences

The pattern will help in establishing results associated with the solution of the research problem in situations where collecting and analyzing data is the only feasible method of validation.

Examples

1. Choobineh and Lo (2005) used an experiment to verify the effectiveness of the proposed system and its improved performance over prior tools; also see Chapter 12, page 202.
2. Purao et al. (2003) conducted a formal experiment to evaluate the performance of the constructed prototype; also see Chapter 12, page 199.

Sources and References

1. Baldwin, D. and Yadav, S. (1995). The Process of Research Investigations in Artificial Intelligence — An Unified View. *IEEE Transactions on Systems*, 25(5), 852–861.
2. Choobineh, J. and Lo, A. (2005). CABSYDD: Case-Based System for Database Design. *Journal of Management Information Systems*, 21(3), 281–314.
3. Purao, S., Storey, V., and Han, T. (2003). Improving Analysis Pattern Reuse in Conceptual Design: Augmenting Automated Processes with Supervised Learning. *Information Systems Research*, 14(3), 269–290.
4. Zelkowitz, M. and Wallace, D. (1998). Experimental Models for Validating Technology. *IEEE Computer*, 31(5), 23–31.

Simulation

Intent

Use simulation to evaluate and validate one's solution to the research problem.

Context and Applicability

The research problem is complex such that one's solution cannot be mathematically proven as valid. The evaluation and validation of the solution in the real-life setting is either not feasible or costly. The problem and its solution can be accurately modeled on a computer.

Description

1. Develop the conceptual model of the problem and its solution that will be simulated on a computer. This will involve deciding what entities and their interactions should be captured in the simulation whose purpose is to evaluate the performance of the solution to the problem and to test its validity.
2. Develop an initial suite of test data that can exercise the model. This must take into account the goals of the solution (artifact) and the outer

environment in which the solution must operate. This will involve modeling the outer environment.

3. Select a simulation package that is specifically designed for the problem domain. This will involve the least amount of programming. If such a package is not available, then choose a general programming language such as C++ or Java and model the problem, solution, and the outer environmental constructs in the language.

4. Run the simulation program for the test suite developed previously. Collect performance data and analyze it to evaluate the solution. If the performance does not meet one's expectations, then one may need to revisit and revise the solution. Otherwise, test the solution over a wide range of conditions. Test the solution on extreme conditions to see the range of outer environmental conditions over which the solution is valid.

5. Argue that the testing is representative of the real-life situations for which the solution is supposed to work. Argue that the data analysis supports the validity of the hypotheses regarding the solution.

Consequences

This pattern, if applicable, provides a reasonable and cost-effective way of evaluating and validating a solution. The alternative of testing the solution in real-life settings may be both costly and time consuming, or may even not be feasible.

Example

1. Vaishnavi et al. (1997) exercised their model using multiple versions of the grocery bagging example; also see "An Example of ICT Design Science Research" in Chapter 2, "Pattern Usage in the Development of the Smart Object Paradigm" in Chapter 5, and Chapter 12, page 189.

Sources and References

1. Simon, H. (1996). *The Sciences of the Artificial*, third edition. Cambridge, MA: MIT Press.
2. Kleindorfer, G., O'Neill, L., and Ganeshan, R. (1998). Validation in Simulation: Various Positions in the Philosophy of Science. *Management Science*, 44(8): 1087–1099.
3. Navidi, W. (2006). *Statistics for Engineers and Scientists*. Boston, MA: McGraw-Hill.

[This text provides an excellent treatment of simulation.]

4. Vaishnavi, V., Buchanan, G., and Kuechler, W. (1997). A Data/Knowledge Paradigm for the Modeling and Design of Operations Support Systems. *IEEE Transactions on Knowledge and Data Engineering*, 9(2), 275–291.

Using Metrics

Intent

Use established metrics to aid validation of one's solution to the research problem.

Context and Applicability

Established metrics exist in the literature that one can use to evaluate the performance of one's solution and to prove or argue the correctness of the hypotheses that one has made regarding the performance of the solution. In case metrics are not available to measure the performance of the solution, one can try using metrics for a similar problem.

Description

1. Determine whether or not there exist established metrics that are appropriate to measure the performance of the solution and to compare it with the performance of previous solutions — if they exist. If such metrics do not exist, determine whether or not metrics exist for measuring the performance of problems similar to one's own problem. In such case, one needs to argue that the use of the chosen metrics is a reasonable way of evaluating and validating one's solution.
2. Analyze or measure the solution using the chosen metrics. This may involve mathematical proofs, experimental measurements, or simulation (see the patterns: *Experimentation*, page 162; *Simulation*, page 164; and *Mathematical Proofs*, page 170).
3. Show that the solution has the hypothesized performance according to the chosen metrics.

Consequences

This pattern allows one to validate the solution in a way that is already accepted by the research community. This makes easier the acceptance of one's solution by the research community.

Examples

1. Using O-notation for expressing the running time or storage use of an algorithm (originally proposed by Knuth) has become an accepted way for theoretically estimating the performance of an algorithm or for comparing

the performance of two algorithms. The metric provides an indication of performance but only for a sufficiently large size of input data and only indicates how the running time (or storage use) will increase as the size of the input data increases. The metric has, however, been well established and accepted by the algorithm analysis and design research community.

2. Vaishnavi et al. (1980) used the well-accepted metric of O-notation to specify the performance of their algorithm; also see Chapter 12, page 216.

3. Datta (1998) proposed and used metrics for the evaluation of the proposed strategies; also see Chapter 12, page 196.

Related Patterns

- Experimentation (page 162)
- Simulation (page 164)
- Mathematical Proofs (page 170)

Sources and References

1. Datta, Anindya. (1998). Automating the Discovery of AS-IS Business Process Models: Probabilistic and Algorithmic Approaches. *Information Systems Research*, 9(3), 275–301.

2. March, S. and Smith, G. (1995). Design and Natural Science Research on Information Technology. *Decision Support Systems*, 15, 251–266.

3. Vaishnavi, V., Kriegel, H., and Wood, D. (1980). Optimum Multiway Search Trees. *Acta Informatica*, 14, 119–133.

Benchmarking

Intent

Use an available benchmark to show that one's solution has reasonable performance or is better than some other available solution.

Context and Applicability

There is no established metric available that one can use to measure the performance of one's solution (see *Using Metrics* pattern, page 166). One would like to show that the performance of one's solution is reasonable or better than some available solution. The research community has, however, developed a benchmark for evaluating solutions to one's class of problems. If no benchmark is available, one can create a test scenario or a class of such scenarios that one can use to evaluate one's solution as well as any other available solution.

Description

1. Identify the benchmark that one can use to evaluate and validate the solution. If no benchmark is available, one can create one's own benchmark. In this case, however, one needs to establish that the benchmark has some independent validity and is not biased toward one's solution.
2. Use the benchmark to show the merit of the solution. If there does not exist any solution to the research problem, then one needs to show that the solution meets the criteria specified in the benchmark for a reasonable solution to the problem. If there exist solutions to the problem, then one needs to show — using the benchmark — that one's own solution is a better solution to the problem than the other existing solutions.

Consequences

Benchmarking provides a vehicle for objective evaluation of a solution or comparison of different solutions. This makes it easy to claim that one has really provided a solution to a problem or to show that one's own solution is better than other existing solutions.

Related Patterns

- Using Metrics (page 166)

Sources and References

1. Tichy, W. (1998). Should Computer Scientists Experiment more? *IEEE Computer*, 31(5), 32–40.
2. Zelkowitz, M. and Wallace, D. (1998). Experimental Models for Validating Technology. *IEEE Computer*, 31(5), 23–31.

Logical Reasoning

Intent

Use logical reasoning to argue the validity of the solution.

Context and Applicability

It is not possible to use a formal mathematical proof to establish the validity of the solution. The problem may be too complex, or it may not be possible to cast the problem and the solution criteria in a formal framework. The constructs and assumptions of the problem are, however, precise enough that a logical argument can be built for the hypothesized claims about the solution. This pattern could serve as a supplement or alternative to the experimental evaluation and validation of the solution.

Description

This is usually a weaker form of validating a solution than either using a mathematical proof or using experimental validation. The steps for this form of validation are:

1. Identify assumptions ("axioms") related to the research problem that are either known to be true or can be argued to be valid assumptions possibly using empirical data.
2. Identify rules ("deduction rules") related to the problem or solution that are either known to be true or can be argued to be valid possibly with the aid of empirical data.
3. Build a logical path from the assumptions (axioms) to the claims one is making about the solution (hypotheses) using the deduction rules one has identified.

Consequences

On the one extreme, when the axioms, deduction rules, and the claims about the solution can be stated precisely and there is no vagueness in showing that the claims follow logically from the axioms, the technique is a mathematical proof for validation (see *Mathematical Proofs* pattern, page 170). On the other extreme, the axioms, the deduction rules, or the logical argumentation may be vague; in this case, the pattern does not serve much value for validation. In this case, one should try the experimental method (*Experimentation* pattern, page 184) or a simulation method (*Simulation* pattern, page 187). There may, however, be a middle ground where this pattern may provide reasonable support for the validation of the proposed solution.

Examples

1. Denning (1968) used logical arguments to argue the usefulness of the entity set model and the correctness of its founding assumptions; also see Chapter 12, page 212.

2. Fraser and Vaishnavi (1997) built a logical argument for showing why a certain strategy should have the potential to result in a certain maturity level of an organization for incorporating formal specifications in its software development process. This provides an internal validation of the proposed model.

3. Hoare (1978) used logical reasoning to motivate CSP and its contribution; also see Chapter 12, page 214.

4. Vaishnavi et al. (1997) provided logical reasons to convince the reader that the paper was making a significant contribution; also see "An Example of ICT Design Science Research" in Chapter 2, "Pattern Usage in the Development of the Smart Object Paradigm" in Chapter 5, and Chapter 12, page 189.

Related Patterns

- Experimentation
- Mathematical Proofs

Sources and References

1. Denning, P. (1968). The Working Set Model for Program Behavior. *Communications of the ACM*, 11(5), 323–333. Reprinted in *Communications of the ACM, 25th Anniversary Issue*, 26(1), 43–48, January 1983.

2. Fraser, M. and Vaishnavi, V. (1997). A Formal Specification Maturity Model. *Communications of the ACM*, 40(12), 95–103.

3. Hoare, C. (1978). Communicating Sequential Processes. *Communications of the ACM*, 21(8), 666–677. Reprinted in *Communications of the ACM, 25th Anniversary Issue*, 26(1), 100–106, January 1983.

4. Vaishnavi, V., Buchanan, G., and Kuechler, W. (1997). A Data/Knowledge Paradigm for the Modeling and Design of Operations Support Systems. *IEEE Transactions on Knowledge and Data Engineering*, 9(2), 275–291.

Mathematical Proofs

Intent

Prove mathematically the claims being made about the solution that one has developed for the research problem.

Context and Applicability

The hypothesized claims for one's solution can be expressed quantitatively, and the essential aspects of the problem and the solution can be expressed formally in a closed logical system.

Description

1. Express the hypothesized claims about the solution quantitatively and precisely.
2. Cast the claim to be proven as a *theorem* in a well-defined, closed formal logical system.
3. Prove any auxiliary results (lemmas) that may aid in proving the theorem about the hypothesized claims about the solution.
4. Prove the claims theorem, possibly using the already-proven lemmas.

Consequences

This pattern provides the strongest form of validation of the claims one has made about the solution. This validation is even stronger than experimental validation (see *Experimentation* pattern, page 162).

Example

1. Vaishnavi et al. (1980) used mathematical proofs to show the correctness and complexity of their proposed algorithm; also see Chapter 12, page 216.

Source and Reference

1. Vaishnavi, V., Kriegel, H., and Wood, D. (1980). Optimum Multiway Search Trees. *Acta Informatica*, 14, 119–133.

Chapter 11

Publishing Patterns

Publishing

The patterns in this chapter are applicable to the Conclusion phase of the research (see Figure 2.5 in Chapter 2). One has either completed a research project or has obtained significant results while conducting research. One would like to write a paper to report one's results.

The following patterns provide guidelines for publication:

- Conference and Journal Submissions
- Writing Conference Papers
- Writing Journal Papers
- ᴹStyle Exemplars
- ᴹAligning with a Paradigm
- Novelty and Significance
- Use of Examples

The *Conference and Journal Submissions* pattern provides general guidelines for submitting papers to conferences and journals, and for deciding whether to write a paper for a conference or a journal.

The *Writing Conference Papers* and *Writing Journal Papers* patterns provide guidelines on how to write papers for conferences and journals, respectively.

The next four patterns— *Style Exemplars, Aligning with a Paradigm, Novelty and Significance*, and *Use of Examples* — provide guidelines that can increase the chances of acceptance of one's paper; it is particularly useful for journal submissions but can also be useful for conference submissions.

Writing research papers for publication is an art. These patterns are an attempt at a brief exposition of this art. The use of the patterns can increase the chances of success of one's writing efforts.

As in previous chapters, the superscript ^M preceding the pattern name indicates a meta-level pattern. The patterns in this chapter — *Style Exemplars* and *Aligning with a Paradigm* — while strongly identified with publication, may in fact also be used at the beginning of a project. Locating an exemplar paper describing research on a closely related topic at the beginning of a project can suggest development methods and validation techniques. Determining the paradigm with which the research problem is most closely associated can also suggest research methods, validation techniques, and allied literature at an early point (just after preliminary problem identification) in the research program.

Conference and Journal Submissions

Intent

Make a judicious choice of a conference or a journal for which one should write a paper.

Context and Applicability

One has completed one's research to solve a certain research problem. Alternatively, one's research is ongoing but has obtained certain results that one would like to report in the form of a paper for a conference or a journal.

Description

Consider writing a paper for a conference when:

- One has obtained some interesting results that one would like to share with the research community without delay.
- One has not yet fully worked out and tested one's solution to the research problem.
- One would like to get feedback from the conference to guide one's further research.

Consider submitting to a journal when:

- One has fully worked out the solution and validated it.
- One's contribution to knowledge is such that it is worth archiving in a journal.

There is significant variety in the standards of conferences and journals. One should carefully choose the conference that best fits the type and quality of the research. For conferences, one should examine prior conference proceedings and "Call for Papers" to find if a certain conference is a suitable outlet for one's work. For journals, examination of past papers and editorial policies can guide the selection process.

Consequences

Conferences and journals have different purposes. By making judicious choices of what work at what stage should be submitted to what conference or journal, one can allow for conference and journal submissions to play a synergistic role in advancing one's research.

Writing Conference Papers

Intent

Write a conference paper.

Context and Applicability

One has decided to write a paper for a conference and has chosen the conference that best suits the intended paper. One would like to know how best to write the paper so that it has the best chance for acceptance.

Description

1. Carefully study the "Call for Papers" to understand the focus of the conference. Identify the topic or track that the paper can fit in. Choose a writing style that best suits the focus of the conference, the chosen topic or track, and the expected audience for the conference.
2. Focus on a single idea to write about in the paper. Fully develop the idea and support it with evidence. The idea should be of potential interest

to the audience and should generate discussion. The topic of the paper should be such that it will add to the value of the conference for the conference attendees.

3. The conference format will not allow for any major revision of the paper in response to the reviewers' comments. Therefore, the paper must be crisp and polished, and needs to meet the specified length restriction for the paper.

4. The paper will be judged on such criteria as originality, technical quality, presentation quality, and contribution or potential impact. Make sure that the paper can score well on such criteria.

5. How a paper should be written also depends on the type of the paper. Here are some examples:

   a. A *theory* paper should have a clear focus; should clearly state the theory, which also must be of interest to the expected conference attendees; should relate the work with existing literature; should provide evidence in support of the theory; and should show that the theory has been tested.

   b. A *methods* paper should clearly provide the goals of the paper, should be focused, should tie the work to related literature, and should defend the proposed method.

   c. An *experience* paper should focus on a single topic, should present relevant facts of an experiential nature, and should advance the state of current knowledge.

Consequences

A successful conference paper can help one obtain timely feedback on research ideas, can help one in socializing with members of one's own research community, and can provide one with new insights and ideas for further development of one's research ideas. In certain cases, a conference paper can also evolve into a journal paper.

Source and Reference

1. Johnson, R.E., Beck, K., Booch, G., Cook, W., Gabriel, R., and Wirfs-Brock, R. (1993). How to Get a Paper Accepted at OOPSLA. *Proceedings of the Eighth Annual Conference on Object Oriented Programming Systems, Languages, and Applications.* New York: ACM Press.

Writing Journal Papers

Intent

Write a journal paper.

Context and Applicability

One has decided to write a paper for a journal and has chosen the journal that best suits the intended paper. One would like to know how best to write the paper so that it has the best chance for acceptance.

Description

1. The journals vary widely in quality, acceptance rates, type of research published, and writing style. Study carefully the editorial policies of the journal and its past papers to write in a way that will be acceptable to the journal.
2. Choose an exemplar paper from the journal that closely matches the intended content of one's own paper. Use this paper as a model to guide the writing of the paper. See the *Style Exemplars* pattern (page 178).
3. If possible, align the paper with a research paradigm that the journal papers share. See the *Aligning with a Paradigm* pattern (page 179).
4. The paper is expected to have novelty and significance. Write the paper in such a way that the novelty and significance of the paper is clearly shown. See the *Novelty and Significance* pattern (p. 181).
5. The acceptance of the paper is based on the report of the referees for the paper. One must make a case to the referees that the paper merits publication in the journal. Write the paper in such a way that it makes this case to the referees.
6. Use examples or preferably a running example that makes the contribution of the paper more understandable. See the *Use of Examples* pattern (p. 183).

Consequences

The paper may be accepted by the journal without any revision or after a minor revision. It is, however, more likely that the paper will be rejected with suggestions for a major revision or conditionally accepted. This is a normal iterative process for journal publications in most cases. In case of a definite rejection, consider rewriting the paper for a different journal.

Related Patterns

- ᴹStyle Exemplars (page 178)
- ᴹAligning with a Paradigm (page 179)
- Novelty and Significance (page 181)
- Use of Examples (page 183)

Example

1. Vaishnavi et al.'s (1997) paper closely followed the principles of writing a paper that has archival value by relating the work to the existing literature and by showing its novelty and significance; also see "An Example of ICT Design Science Research" in Chapter 2, "Pattern Usage in the Development of the Smart Object Paradigm" in Chapter 5, and Chapter 12, page 189.

Sources and References

1. Vaishnavi, V., Buchanan, G., and Kuechler, W. (1997). A Data/Knowledge Paradigm for the Modeling and Design of Operations Support Systems. *IEEE Transactions on Knowledge and Data Engineering*, 9(2), 275–291.

ᴹStyle Exemplars

Intent

Use a style exemplar to increase the chances of success for the acceptance of one's paper.

Context and Applicability

One is trying to write a paper to report research that is of good quality. However, the quality of the reported research by itself does not guarantee publication success. One would like to write the paper in such a way that it is well received by the referees while it is being reviewed, and by the audience after it is published.

Description

1. Find an exemplar paper in the journal that is close to the contents of one's intended paper. Ideally, the authors of the exemplar paper should be well established and recognized by the research community.
2. Use the exemplar paper as a model to guide the writing of one's own paper. Use the notation and style of the exemplar paper to the extent possible and adapt it minimally if needed.

Consequences

The use of this pattern will help one to write a paper in a manner that is likely to be well received by the referees of the paper and thus accepted by them. It also helps readers better understand the paper because it lets them understand the paper in the context of notation and style that is likely already familiar to them.

Examples

1. Vaishnavi et al. (1997) used this meta-level pattern in the Evaluation phase of their research to model the validation portion of their research after existing papers that also used demonstration for validation; also see "An Example of ICT Design Science Research" in Chapter 2, "Pattern Usage in the Development of the Smart Object Paradigm" in Chapter 5, and Chapter 12, page 189.
2. Vaishnavi et al. (1980) modeled their paper after the one written by Knuth for the same journal and for solving a similar problem for binary search trees; also see "An Example of ICT Design Science Research" in Chapter 2, "Pattern Usage in the Development of the Smart Object Paradigm" in Chapter 5, and Chapter 12, page 216.

Sources and References

1. Vaishnavi, V., Buchanan, G., and Kuechler, W. (1997). A Data/Knowledge Paradigm for the Modeling and Design of Operations Support Systems. *IEEE Transactions on Knowledge and Data Engineering*, 9(2), 275–291.
2. Vaishnavi, V., Kriegel, H., and Wood, D. (1980). Optimum Multiway Search Trees. *Acta Informatica*, 14, 119–133.

ᴹAligning with a Paradigm

Intent

Write the paper in such a way that it aligns with a research paradigm shared by the publication outlet.

Context and Applicability

One has identified a publication outlet such as a journal for which one would like to write a paper to report the research. One would like to do it in such a way that the paper is well received by the research community.

Description

Acceptance of research by the research community is a *social* process. The way people in the research community understand and react to a new research paper is heavily affected by the prevailing research paradigms. These paradigms contribute to shared symbols, beliefs, research puzzles, analogies, and metaphors, which in turn determine the importance of research questions and acceptance of explanations provided in a paper.

Writing a research paper in such a way that it aligns with the prevailing research paradigm (or paradigms) increases the chances of acceptance of the paper by the research community. The alignment can be in terms of the research issues raised, the approach for addressing the research issues, or the way the research is presented. Not all the research need to or should follow the existing paradigms; never departing from the prevailing paradigms would be detrimental to the advancement of a field. It, however, takes a greater effort to get acceptance of a paper from the research community if the paper significantly departs from the prevailing research paradigms.

The following steps can help in understanding the prevailing research paradigms and in writing a paper in a way that aligns with such paradigms:

1. Take time to fully comprehend the prevailing research paradigms in the area of one's own research. The *Understanding Research Community* (page 112) pattern can be useful in this task.
2. Relate the research problem to the research issues that the research community already understands.
3. Use the community's shared symbols and beliefs in writing a paper.
4. Find exemplar papers and then model the paper after those exemplar papers. See the *Style Exemplars* pattern (page 178).

Consequences

The use of this pattern will maximize the chances of acceptance of the paper. One need not always use this pattern. One can choose to write a paper that departs from the prevailing paradigms but one should make a conscious decision to that effect. In such a case, the paper needs to educate the reader about the presented concepts and at least relate them to what the reader is expected to already know.

Examples

1. Hoare (1978) presented communicating sequential processes in a manner that aligns it with the shared symbols and beliefs of the research community that deals with formal treatment of parallel programming; also see Chapter 12, page 214.

2. Vaishnavi et al. (1997) reviewed literature to align their work with respect to existing paradigms and also used this meta-level pattern in the Awareness of Problem phase of their research; also see "An Example of ICT Design Science Research" in Chapter 2, "Pattern Usage in the Development of the Smart Object Paradigm" in Chapter 5, and Chapter 12, page 189.

Related Patterns

- Understanding Research Community
- ^MStyle Exemplars

Sources and References

1. Hoare, C. (1978). Communicating Sequential Processes. *Communications of the ACM*, 21(8), 666–677. Reprinted in *Communications of the ACM, 25th Anniversary Issue*, 26(1), 100–106, January 1983.
2. Kuhn, T. (1996). *The Structure of Scientific Revolutions*, third edition, Chicago: The University of Chicago Press.
3. Vaishnavi, V., Buchanan, G., and Kuechler, W. (1997). A Data/Knowledge Paradigm for the Modeling and Design of Operations Support Systems. *IEEE Transactions on Knowledge and Data Engineering*, 9(2), 275–291.

Novelty and Significance

Intent

Make sure that the paper shows both novelty and significance.

Context and Applicability

One has conducted research that has both novelty and significance. One would like to write the paper in such a way that the reviewers of the paper clearly see both.

Description

A paper submitted to a journal or conference should be written for the reviewers of the paper as well as for the general readers of the paper after publication. It is the reviewers (referees) who decide whether to accept or reject the paper for publication. The reviewers are likely to be less familiar with the specific research problem than the paper's author. It is one's own responsibility to show clearly the novelty and significance of the research so that the paper is not rejected on those grounds. Here are some guidelines in this area:

- Place the research in the context of the existing literature showing novelty and significance. Show clearly the knowledge gaps in the existing literature. Discuss the importance of these gaps. Discuss how one's reported research fills these gaps. The introduction is usually the section to establish the novelty and significance of the research. The significance of the reported research should also be highlighted in the concluding section of the paper.
- Discuss the potential limitations of the research and topics of future research in the concluding section. This helps in preventing any false impression about the contribution of the reported research.

Consequences

The use of this pattern can help the reviewers of the paper gain a better understanding of the novelty and contribution of the paper. This, in turn, can improve the chances of the paper's acceptance for publication.

Examples

1. Codd (1970) showed the novelty and significance of his work by discussing his work in the context of problems in existing data models and their significance; also see Chapter 12, page 209.
2. Denning (1968) showed novelty and significance by contrasting the proposed model with existing models and by showing how this work initiates a new direction of research in system resource allocation; also see Chapter 12, page 212.
3. Hoare's paper (1978) demonstrated its novelty by comparing the reported research with existing research in the area. It showed its significance by showing that a small number of concepts — input, output, and concurrency — can be regarded as primitive concepts of parallel programming; also see Chapter 12, page 214.
4. Parao et al. (2003) stressed the novelty of the approach used and the significance of the problem addressed throughout the paper; also see Chapter 12, page 199.
5. Vaishnavi et al.'s paper (1997) showed the novelty and significance of the reported work by discussing its strengths and limitations in the context of the existing literature; also see "An Example of ICT Design Science Research" in Chapter 2, "Pattern Usage in the Development of the Smart Object Paradigm" in Chapter 5, and Chapter 12, page 189.

6. Because the reported work (Vaishnavi et al., 1980) is solving a problem for multiway search trees that is similar to the one previously solved by Knuth, the authors carefully distinguished the two problems and also showed that a simple generalization of Knuth's solution is not an efficient solution to the problem; also see Chapter 12, page 216.

Sources and References

1. Codd, E.F. (1970). A Relational Model of Data for Large Shared Data Banks. *Communications of the ACM*, 13(6), 377–387. Reprinted in *Communications of the ACM, 25th Anniversary Issue*, 26(1), 64–69, January 1983.
2. Denning, P. (1968). The Working Set Model for Program Behavior. *Communications of the ACM*, 11(5), 323–333. Reprinted in *Communications of the ACM, 25th Anniversary Issue*, 26(1), 43–48, January 1983.
3. Hoare, C. (1978). Communicating Sequential Processes. *Communications of the ACM*, 21(8), 666–677. Reprinted in *Communications of the ACM, 25th Anniversary Issue*, 26(1), 100–106, January 1983.
4. Purao, S., Storey, V., and Han, T. (2003). Improving Analysis Pattern Reuse in Conceptual Design: Augmenting Automated Processes with Supervised Learning. *Information Systems Research*, 14(3), 269–290.
5. Vaishnavi, V., Buchanan, G., and Kuechler, W. (1997). A Data/Knowledge Paradigm for the Modeling and Design of Operations Support Systems. *IEEE Transactions on Knowledge and Data Engineering*, 9(2), 275–291.
6. Vaishnavi, V., Kriegel, H., and Wood, D. (1980). Optimum Multiway Search Trees. *Acta Informatica*, 14, 119–133.

Use of Examples

Intent

Use concrete examples to provide a better understanding of the research.

Context and Applicability

One's research solves a general research problem that has applications to a class of problems. By staying at too general a level, the readers may not be able to fully understand the reported research or its benefits.

Description

1. Use a running example or a number of related examples to provide concrete illustrations of one's research and its benefits.

2. Use each example to illustrate a distinct aspect of one's research and its benefits.
3. Describe the purpose of each example and how it is achieving its purpose.
4. Use graphics, where applicable, to improve the message of an example.

Consequences

The use of this pattern can improve the readability of a paper. The readability of the paper can also be beneficial in the publication review process.

Examples

1. Chen (1976) used a running example to illustrate the proposed model and diagrammatic technique; also see Chapter 12, page 207.
2. Codd's paper (1970) contains a parts-projects-suppliers example to illustrate the relational model and its benefits; also see Chapter 12, page 209.
3. Hoare (1978) uses a number of well-known examples to demonstrate the use of the concepts in CSP; also see Chapter 12, page 214.
4. Purao et al. (2003) used a running example to illustrate the proposed model and diagrammatic technique; also see Chapter 12, page 199.
5. Vaishnavi et al.'s paper (1997) contains a number of examples to show the concepts related to the smart object model and to show their novelty and significance; also see "An Example of ICT Design Science Research" in Chapter 2, "Pattern Usage in the Development of the Smart Object Paradigm" in Chapter 5, and Chapter 12, page 189.

Sources and References

1. Chen, P. (1976). The Entity-Relationship Model: Toward a Unified View of Data. *ACM Transactions on Database Systems*, 1(1), 9–37.
2. Codd, E.F. (1970). A Relational Model of Data for Large Shared Data Banks. *Communications of the ACM*, 13(6), 377–387. Reprinted in *Communications of the ACM, 25th Anniversary Issue*, 26(1), 64–69, January 1983.
3. Hoare, C. (1978). Communicating Sequential Processes. *Communications of the ACM*, 21(8), 666–677. Reprinted in *Communications of the ACM, 25th Anniversary Issue*, 26(1), 100–106, January 1983.
4. Purao, S., Storey, V., and Han, T. (2003). Improving Analysis Pattern Reuse in Conceptual Design: Augmenting Automated Processes with Supervised Learning. *Information Systems Research*, 14(3), 269–290.
5. Vaishnavi, V., Buchanan, G., and Kuechler, W. (1997). A Data/Knowledge Paradigm for the Modeling and Design of Operations Support Systems. *IEEE Transactions on Knowledge and Data Engineering*, 9(2), 275–291.

RESEARCH PATTERN
USAGE EXEMPLARS

Chapter 12

Pattern Analysis of Design Science Research Exemplars

Pattern Analysis

In this chapter, published design science research papers, many of which have been highly influential in their areas, are analyzed in terms of the patterns used in the performance of the research effort they describe. Some of the papers are from the information systems (IS) area while others are from the related field of computer science. In either case, they are exemplars of *learning and investigation through artifact construction*, the most fundamental characteristic of design science research.

The chapter is useful for several modes of learning about design science research (DSR). The chapter can be scanned for examples of patterns the reader may wish to investigate further. The patterns for a particular analysis are grouped into the classifications used in prior chapters and in frameworks throughout this book. After identifying patterns of interest, the papers containing those patterns can be read in detail to see how, in actual practice in a research context, the patterns were executed. Alternatively, one or more of the analyzed papers can be read in full — possibly chosen for the reader's interest in or knowledge of a certain area — and then the pattern analysis can be followed on a second reading of the research paper.

While this chapter concludes the book, the authors sincerely hope it does not conclude the reader's interest in or pursuit of design science research. An excellent way of proceeding from this chapter in a research methods course would be to immediately choose examples of design research from IS or related fields other than those analyzed in this book and proceed with an analysis on these papers similar to the analyses in this chapter. It is not significant to the learning process if the reader has no familiarity with the actual detailed processes that occurred in the research effort described. As discussed at other points in the book, published descriptions of research usually focus on the results of the research — not the process. What is important is identification of the patterns and processes that are applicable or might have been at work in the research effort. These patterns can be identified by a hermeneutic* reading of the paper while (1) continually referring to the general methodology of design research framework (Figure 2.5 in Chapter 2) as the overall activity flow that is most likely to have occurred, and (2) referring to the patterns applicable to each of the general design methodology framework phases.

For example, the patterns used to identify and refine a problem area are frequently visible (between the lines) in the Introduction section of the paper and sometimes the Literature Review section. Research paper authors are frequently at some pains to justify the contribution of their literature to a research area, and the patterns used both to align with a research community and to define and refine their problem area can sometimes be identified in the Conclusion sections of the paper as well as the sections just mentioned. Similarly, the patterns used to arrive at a successful validation effort can frequently be detected in the Discussion sessions of many research papers.

Additional insights into design science research can be gained by interviewing or even casually speaking with researchers in the midst of a current design science research project. The patterns and the general design science research methodology of Figure 2.5 in Chapter 2 can be the basis for formal or informal discussions with researchers. Ultimately, a full understanding of the design science research method can only be obtained through participation in a project using this methodology. However, a technique that approximates the performance of research and is more amenable to a research methods course is the preparation of a detailed proposal for a design science research project. This technique has been used with success for a number of years in courses in the Information Systems Ph.D. program at Georgia State University.

---

* Hermeneutics means the interpretation and understanding of social events by analyzing their meanings to the human participants and their *culture*. It differs from other interpretative techniques in that it emphasizes the importance of the content as well as the form of any given social behavior. The central principle of hermeneutics is that it is only possible to grasp the meaning of an action or statement by relating it to the whole discourse or world-view from which it originates; for example, putting a piece of paper in a box might be considered a meaningless action unless put in the context of democratic elections, and the action of putting a ballot paper in a box. One can frequently find reference to the "hermeneutic circle," that is, relating the whole to the part and the part to the whole (excerpted from the Wikipedia entry for *hermeneutics*).

The following published works have been mined for patterns:

- "A Data/Knowledge Paradigm for the Modeling and Design of Operations Support Systems" (also see " An Example of ICT Design Science Research" in Chapter 2)
- "Automating the Discovery of AS-IS Business Process Models: Probabilistic and Algorithmic Approaches"
- "Improving Analysis Pattern Reuse in Conceptual Design: Augmenting Automated Processes with Supervised Learning"
- "CABSYDD: Case-Based System for Database Design"
- "World Wide Web: Proposal for Hypertext Project"
- "The Entity-Relationship Model: Toward a Unified View of Data"
- "A Relational Model of Data for Large Shared Data Banks"
- "The Working Set Model for Program Behavior"
- "Communicating Sequential Processes"
- "Optimum Multiway Search Trees"

Note: The analysis of the first and the last papers reflects the authors' perspective because of their personal association with the research reported in those papers.

"A Data/Knowledge Paradigm for the Modeling and Design of Operations Support Systems"

Source

Vaishnavi, V., Buchanan, G., and Kuechler, W. (1997). A Data/Knowledge Paradigm for the Modeling and Design of Operations Support Systems. *IEEE Transactions on Knowledge and Data Engineering*, 9(2), 275–291.

Problem Selection and Development Patterns (Awareness of Problem Phase)

Aligning with a Paradigm

Smart objects began with the recognition of the problem of control of a complex environment as amenable to a design research solution. All authors understood the design science research (DSR) paradigm from years of research or practical experience in the design field, and proceeded more deeply in their initial investigations only after having identified the nuclear power control problem as a DSR opportunity, implicitly utilizing this meta-level pattern.

Solution Scope Mismatch

The research problem was identified while attempting to develop a support system for a nuclear reactor using the rule-based language, Prolog. The authors soon realized that it would be nearly impossible to develop such a system in Prolog and to maintain it to support the thousands of procedures typically needed in a commercial nuclear power plant. This led, in turn, to the realization that the current tools were not fully capable of constructing and continuously maintaining a support system for the operation of a complex environment. This meta-level pattern was also used in the Suggestion phase of the research while attempting to find an appropriate solution to the research problem.

Being Visionary (and Brainstorming)

The authors analyzed the best available solutions (design, data, and knowledge models) with respect to the problem of modeling complex systems and found them to be not fully suitable. They then envisioned an improvement in the situation by coming up with a set of attributes that they felt were essential to any conceptual model of operations support systems. The attributes of this process that distinguish it from design per se is that the authors knew, as they were developing the attribute set, that no existing technology could meet the requirements. This type of envisioning is sometimes termed "blue sky" design and effectively merges with the actions for the *Brainstorming* pattern. This meta-level pattern was also used in the Development phase of the research in attempting to find a novel solution.

Bridging Research Communities

The researchers identified three distinct but interrelated research communities — software engineering, database systems, and knowledge based systems — that have developed distinct approaches to addressing the problem of modeling complex systems, none of which was adequate to the problem by itself. After familiarizing themselves with concepts from object-oriented design, semantic data modeling, active database system modeling, and rule-based knowledge modeling, they then identified attributes in each model essential for the design of complex systems and synthesized these in a complementary manner to develop the smart object model. The identification of and analysis of the three research communities required the use of the closely related patterns (to Bridging Research Communities):

- Problem Area Identification
- Research Conversation (this meta-level pattern was also used in the Suggestion and Development phases of the research)
- Research Domain Identification (also used in Conclusion phase)

- Understanding Research Community
- Problem Formulation

Complex System Analysis

The authors analyzed the systems dealing with the management of complex operations environments, which they termed "operations support systems" (OSS). As such, no traditional class of information systems had the capability to address the depth of interactive, global support required for managing operations environments, so they began by identifying the functionality required to improve the effectiveness of systems for managing operations environments. This meta-level pattern was also used in the Suggestion phase of the research to analyze an initial solution based on the use of frames for knowledge representation.

Literature Search Patterns (Awareness of Problem Phase)

Industry and Practice Awareness

This meta-level pattern was used both in the Problem Awareness and Conclusion Suggestion phases of the research. The authors identified problems faced in practice and abstracted them into research problems when they attempted to model a complex operations environment with Prolog; see "An Example of ICT Design Science Research" in Chapter 2. Using this "hands-on" approach, they increased their awareness of developments and problems in industry and practice, and also experienced them first-hand.

Suggestion and Development Patterns (Suggestion and Development Phases)

Theory Development

The authors formally stated their theory of the smart object paradigm, which was a conceptual framework, and its instantiation, the smart object model (SOM), as a new model for modeling complex operations support systems.

Approaches to Building Theory

The authors used the hypothetical and deductive approach to building theory using intuition, results of past experimentation, a literature review of approaches in different research communities such as data and knowledge models, etc. to develop a new solution, the smart object paradigm, and the associated theory.

Problem Space Tools and Techniques, and Research Community Tools and Techniques

The authors analyzed existing tools and techniques, abstracted relevant concepts, and incorporated those concepts into the smart object paradigm framework.

Abstracting Concepts

The attribute set required by the model (see discussion on "Being Visionary," above) was derived by abstracting general control principles from multiple examples of operations control environments and multiple partial solutions to the problem (see also "Combining Partial Solutions").

Elegant Design

The artifact (here, SOM, an instantiation of the smart object paradigm) is designed to be general and could be defined in functional terms. The model underlying the artifact is independent of its outer and inner environments and thus can be used to manage any operations environment. The authors also mentioned that the paradigm has proven richer than anticipated because it could be used in applications beyond its original intent.

Hierarchical Design

In developing the smart object model, Vaishnavi et al. decomposed the problem into sub-parts. First, the smart object paradigm framework was described. Second, the logical and architectural views were reviewed. Then the steps to transition from the smart object paradigm to a working operations support system (OSS) were defined. The authors then decomposed the model into its conceptual attributes and its functional attributes. The problem of defining the conceptual attributes and functional attributes was further decomposed into sub-problems. For example, conceptual attributes were decomposed into sub-attributes of knowledge associated with operations, adaptive inferencing, structural relations between operations, etc. These attributes were further decomposed into lower-level problems. The complexity of the problem was both defined and appropriately handled by this approach.

Combining Partial Solutions and Sketching Solutions

The authors found that while semantic data models, rule-based inferencing models, and object-oriented design provided partial solutions for operations support systems, they did not address all the desired attributes — particularly control abstraction. Using the *Sketching Solutions* pattern, they identified the need to combine the strengths of the partial solutions augmented with the concept of a monitor to form the complete solution.

Interdisciplinary Solution Extrapolation

The smart object paradigm fuses together concepts from databases, software engineering, artificial intelligence, and operating systems. It uses the general object-oriented structure from software engineering to manage complexity, semantic data modeling concepts from databases, and production systems from artificial intelligence (AI), along with the operating systems concept of using a stack to monitor the status of an object.

General Solution Principle

The authors identified a general problem — the support of complex, large operations environments. They developed a general solution — the OSS framework — that can be instantiated for specific situations. The general solution is so broad that it can be called a paradigm. At various stages in developing this solution, the following meta-level patterns were used:

- Different Perspectives
- Means-Ends Analysis
- Cost-Benefit Analysis

Integrating Techniques

The concept of a smart object model draws conceptual modeling techniques from semantic data modeling, production systems, and the object modeling areas. It integrates into the model functionality from data modeling and knowledge engineering areas. It additionally introduces the concept of a "monitor" that helps in integrating the various techniques and creating a model that meets the desired requirements.

Using Human Roles

When the authors were surveying nuclear power plants and other complex operations environments, one of the primary shortcomings of existing attempts at computer control was that they were partial and required large amounts of human assistance. The authors analyzed the role played by human judgment in these environments and determined that much of it could be assumed by a meta-level of rules performing the human supervisory tasks.

Evaluation and Validation Patterns (Evaluation Phase)

Technological Approach Exemplars

The *Technological Approach Exemplars* pattern led to a review of the problem domain literature focused on discovering what validation techniques were used by the chosen research community. This information did not absolutely constrain the direction taken but definitely influenced it; it is widely understood that straying beyond the techniques commonly employed by a research community increases the difficulty of publishing in that community.

Demonstration

The authors evaluated the modeling ability of the smart object model by demonstrating its use for part of an operations support system for the nuclear power plant, which motivated the entire work. They also used the widely understood grocery bagging example from artificial intelligence (AI) to show the power of the model.

Simulation

The demonstration of the smart object model using the grocery bagging example is extensive enough to be considered a simulation. Every aspect of the model is exercised in some manner in the demonstration.

Logical Reasoning

The authors did not provide any mathematical proofs but did provide logical arguments to substantiate that the presented model is better able to model complex environments. They also argued that the model is conceptually consistent and maintainable. They presented their case in the background of the existing literature in the related areas. They made the case that the presented work draws from the existing knowledge base and, in turn, contributes new knowledge.

Cost-Benefit Analysis

This meta-level pattern was used to determine the best strategy to use for the evaluation of the research.

Publishing Patterns (Conclusion Phase)

Aligning with a Paradigm

The paper provides an extensive literature review to motivate the work and to align and relate it to the existing paradigms. It also discusses and illustrates the presented concepts in light of the existing literature, showing both novelty and significance.

Research Conversation

Closely related to the *Aligning with a Paradigm* pattern, this meta-level pattern was used to more specifically position the paper by identifying a journal that contained an ongoing research conversation into which this research could logically enter. Research conversation in this sense refers to multiple papers in multiple issues of the same journal cumulatively approaching a comprehensive solution to a large problem by presenting solutions to various aspects of the problem.

Writing Journal Papers

This paper was written at the conclusion of an extensive, four-year research program. The results of the research were solid enough and had been previewed and accepted at several conferences such that the chances for publication of a well-written journal paper were good. The conference papers, in turn, productively used the *Writing Conference Papers* pattern.

Novelty and Significance

The paper demonstrates novelty and significance by showing that the existing models drawn from a number of areas do not provide a total solution to the problem of modeling complex operations support systems and showing how the presented work fills an important knowledge gap. By placing the work in the context of the existing literature and showing its similarities and differences with existing models, along with discussing the limitations of the work, the authors bring out the novel and significant aspects of the work.

Use of Examples

This paper contains a number of examples related to a subsystem of a prototype for an operations support system for a nuclear power plant to illustrate the concepts as well as to demonstrate the modeling capability of the smart object model.

Style Exemplars

While the authors did not use any single paper as a template for the presentation of their ideas, they did search the target journal for, and found, multiple papers that presented novel, well-developed theoretical solutions to complex problems. These papers also relied on demonstration for validation, just as their paper, and provided style guidance in the writing of the paper.

"Automating the Discovery of AS-IS Business Process Models: Probabilistic and Algorithmic Approaches"

Source

Datta, A. (1998). Automating the Discovery of AS-IS Business Process Models: Probabilistic and Algorithmic Approaches. *Information Systems Research*, 9(3), 275–301.

Problem Selection and Development Patterns (Awareness of Problem Phase)

Note: The author posed a problem toward which no prior work has been directed. For this reason, more effort is taken to justify the value to practice of the problem and the approach to its solution than would be necessary for the presentation of research that incrementally advances the solution to a previously researched (and acknowledged as important) problem.

Problem Formulation

The paper begins by identifying a previously unarticulated problem. The problem is inferred from the literature on workflow management, business process reengineering, and organizational management, where the *assumption* has been made that AS-IS processes (i.e., processes currently in use) are known. The paper first develops the case that, in practice, AS-IS processes are frequently *not* known and are expensive to determine. Then the concept of a process activity graph (PAG) is defined carefully as a partial but extremely important part of the solution of the problem. An entire section (Section 3) is devoted to defining and defending the utility of PAGs.

Bridging Research Communities

The research drew heavily from the communities of workflow management, business process reengineering, and grammar discovery, as previously applied to software process discovery. The author acknowledged the degree to which prior research in software process discovery informs the presented research.

Structuring an Ill-Structured Problem

The problem of the automated discovery of complete process descriptions from actual process event traces is extremely difficult. The paper approached this by decomposing the total problem into components and demonstrating that a PAG (which the research presented in the paper is able to discover) is a vital and necessary component of a total automated discovery of AS-IS processes. [Speculating from experience, the authors of this book wonder if perhaps Section 3 of the paper, a careful development of and defense of the PAG as a necessary component of a complete process description, was not necessitated by reviewer comments of an earlier draft. That is, the research the authors present automates the discovery of PAGs from process event traces. This is not a complete solution to the problem of the automated discovery of business processes, and early reviews of the paper may have required the authors to defend the significance of their contribution. In so doing, a more structured view of the overall problem was introduced. Whether or not Section 3 was actually so motivated, the after-the-fact defense of a research contribution in response to reviewer comments is quite common and frequently has a constructive result.]

Interdisciplinary Problem Extrapolation

Work from the related area of software process discovery on the use of grammar discovery to reveal processes maps from event traces strongly informs this research.

Literature Search Patterns (Awareness of Problem Phase)

Note that there is no explicit literature review section in this paper. Instead, the relevant and supporting literature is introduced into the discussions of the appropriate sections. Section 3 introduces citations to support the adequacy of the PAG for modeling business processes. In Section 4, the process discovery strategies presented in the paper are grounded in prior cited work on grammar discovery. In Section 6, the basis for the algorithmic model of process discovery introduced in the paper (one of two novel discovery methods) is grounded in the literature.

Framework Development

The literature supporting the research draws from multiple fields, none of which address the exact problem to which the research proposes a partial solution. Thus, it is necessary for the author to create an intellectual structure for the work, more carefully developing the point of departure for the research than would be necessary for a previously researched problem.

Industry and Practice Awareness

Throughout Sections 1 and 2 of the paper, the author repeatedly stressed the real-world aspects of the problem addressed by the research, bolstered by frequent general citations from workflow and process management, that is, citations not directly supporting the technical aspects of the research contribution.

Suggestion and Development Patterns (Suggestion and Development Phases)

Note: There is quite a bit of synthesis in this paper, as would be expected when the research contribution is directed toward a novel problem.

Combining Partial Solutions

The research draws heavily from prior work in software process discovery using grammar discovery. The problem addressed is, however, sufficiently different that additional techniques such as Markov chain modeling and finite state machine synthesis need to be incorporated into the final solution.

Interdisciplinary Solution Extrapolation

As previously mentioned, work from multiple fields — process modeling, workflow management, computer science (finite state machines), and operations research (Markov chain modeling) — is recognized as a necessary component of the research solution.

Abstracting Concepts

The research hinges on the author's ability to recognize a basis for a solution to the problem the research addresses in the prior work on software process modeling via grammar discovery. The prior work is abstracted to a general approach to analogous problems.

Integrating Techniques

Work from the multiple fields previously mentioned not only grounds and supports the approach, but is drawn into a complex synthesis to provide three novel approaches to real-world process discovery from event traces.

Evaluation and Validation Patterns (Evaluation Phase)

Note: The problem addressed is complex and does not lend itself to closed form solutions. Furthermore, the author's probabilistic approach in itself precludes formal proofs of correctness. Thus, the research contribution is partially validated with reasoning and a case walk-through (demonstration).

Logical Reasoning

In Section 7, the author sets forth metrics for evaluation of the process discovery strategies. The metrics themselves could be problematic; however, the author relies on "self-evident reasonableness" as a validation of the metrics. The way in which these metrics are potentially satisfied by the strategies is discussed.

Demonstration

Section 8 shows that the metrics introduced in the previous section are satisfied in a walk-through of a simple case to which they have been applied. The merits of the PAGs generated by the different strategies relative to the metrics are discussed.

"Improving Analysis Pattern Reuse in Conceptual Design: Augmenting Automated Processes with Supervised Learning"

Source

Purao, S., Storey, V., and Han, T. (2003). Improving Analysis Pattern Reuse in Conceptual Design: Augmenting Automated Processes with Supervised Learning. *Information Science Research*, 14(3), 269–290.

Problem Selection and Development Patterns (Awareness of Problem Phase)

Problem Formulation

The problem is identified in the literature from information systems and software engineering and from unanswered questions from the author's prior research in related areas. It is clearly stated and scoped. The difference between the approach presented in the paper and prior (naïve) approaches is clearly delineated and used to help define the problem.

Leveraging Expertise

The problems and approaches to their solution were familiar to several of the authors from prior research.

Bridging Research Communities

The research draws heavily from the communities of software engineering, machine learning, and human learning and cognition.

Structuring an Ill-Structured Problem

Drawing heavily from the well-researched machine learning community generates a structured approach to the complex and not well-understood problem of duplicating expert performance in conceptual design.

Literature Search Patterns (Awareness of Problem Phase)

Industry and Practice Awareness

What motivated the research was the longstanding industry problem of facilitating the reuse of design components.

Framework Development

The approach to the problem began with the development of a framework of machine learning techniques.

Suggestion and Development Patterns (Suggestion and Development Phases)

Empirical Refinement

Plans for future work indicated plans for refinement and empirical observation.

General Solution Principle

The prototype design-assist mechanism is very general, capable of enhanced and naïve modes, and of trained or untrained modes within the broader enhanced mode.

Interdisciplinary Solution Extrapolation

Use of machine learning techniques to enhance information retrieval has been explored in multiple fields, including Web search. Here, that general solution technique was applied to conceptual design reuse.

Problem Space Tools and Techniques

One of the prominent activities of this pattern is to "see if there is a promising tool or technique that has been overlooked by the research community" (page 126). Inclusion of machine learning to instantiate theories of expert cognition in the design area exemplifies that approach.

Evaluation and Validation Patterns (Evaluation Phase)

Demonstration

This paper demonstrated the solution through the construction and exercise of a prototype. The demonstration proceeded through a proof-of-concept feasibility study.

Experimentation

Following the feasibility demonstration, a formal experiment was conducted to evaluate the performance of the prototype. (*Note*: The construction of a prototype, followed by both proof-of-concept and formal experimental validation, is rare for the type of complex artifact found in this paper and in the ICT design research communities in general.)

Publishing Patterns (Conclusion Phase)

Use of Examples

This paper used a running example to illustrate the proposed model and diagrammatic technique. The training of the machine learning modules in the proof-of-concept phase introduced the cases and databases used in the later experiment.

Novelty and Significance

Beginning with the abstract, this paper stressed the novelty of its approach in solving a significant problem. The themes were reinforced throughout the paper.

"A Case-Based Database Design Support System"

Source

Choobineh, J. and Lo, A. (2005). CABSYDD: Case-Based System for Database Design. *Journal of Management Information Systems*, 21(3), 281–314.

Problem Selection and Development Patterns (Awareness of Problem Phase)

Leveraging Expertise

The authors had worked together before on survey research in the same field (database design support systems). Beginning research in a new field with a survey paper to become familiar with the field and possibly determine gaps in the literature is a very productive strategy.

Research Conversation

Their prior survey work in the field allowed the authors to identify a research conversation — automated database design support systems — in which to participate. This positions them in a paradigmatic community as researchers who are familiar with the problems and techniques of exploring the problems in this area, who perceive the problems as important, and whose prior research provides grounding for the current research. Assuming reasonable novelty for the new contribution, publication is easier than is usually the case for research in new fields or on problems not previously identified.

Experimentation and Exploration

The authors chose to frame their "problem" — more effective database design tools — in the context of an existing, published system: NAICS (North American Industry Classification System). This contributed to an understanding of the problem and the contribution by the research community, as well as providing a firm point of comparison for later evaluation and validation.

Literature Search Patterns (Awareness of Problem Phase)

Note that there is no formal literature search section in this paper. Instead, supporting citations are introduced as the approach to the problem (well known within the community addressed) is developed. In the concluding section, the contribution of the paper is compared to other published contributions. Placing the comparison at the end of the paper, instead of contrasting the approach to prior work at the beginning of the paper, is unusual but works well for an incremental contribution to an acknowledged difficult problem.

Understanding Research Community

A thorough understanding of the research community the authors are addressing has come from their prior survey work in the area. Notice how patterns in various sections of research development (problem selection, literature search, etc.) interleave, as would be expected when the patterns form a true "pattern language."

Suggestion and Development Patterns (Suggestion and Development Phases)

Research Community Tools and Techniques

The previous survey of the field performed by the authors provided them with an overview of the primary techniques in use: prototype building followed by experimental validation.

Incremental Theory Development

The authors took the primary technique of the research community, prototype construction of expert design support systems, and added the incremental novelty of a case-based approach to the prior work based on first principles of database design. This logically channels the evaluation of the prototype (see patterns below) into a comparison of the prior and novel developments.

Evaluation and Validation Patterns (Evaluation Phase)

Demonstration

Similar to many of the problems addressed in design science research, the optimal design of a database support system is complex; even the concept of optimal is subject to contextual interpretation. For this reason, strong methods of proof are not widely applicable, and demonstration and empirical verification are common. Note the authors' careful delineation of *validation* and *verification* in the section entitled "Evaluation of the Systems." They *validated* the system by expert evaluation of a demonstration of the system for two expert database designers. Verification is a separate step involving a different but related pattern (below).

Experimentation

The effectiveness of the system is *verified* by an experiment. To demonstrate the improved performance of their advance over prior tools, the authors conducted an experiment involving analysis of the performance of 31 students' use of a case-based and theory-based design prototype.

"World Wide Web: Proposal for Hypertext Project"

Source

Berners-Lee, T. and Cailliau, R. (1990). WorldWideWeb: Proposal for a Hypertext Project. http://www.w3.org/Proposal.html.

Note: The source above is not a research publication in a refereed journal or the proceedings of a conference; rather, it is a proposal that was submitted by Berners-Lee and Cailliau to CERN (The European Center for Nuclear Research). CERN is the world's largest particle physics research center where scientists conduct experiments using particle accelerators and detectors to study the smallest constituents of matter to answer questions about the origins of matter and the universe. The reason we have included the proposal is its importance. It was the seed that led to the creation of the World Wide Web. The Web site for CERN, <http://public.web.cern.ch/Public /Welcome.html>, rightly paraphrases the introduction of CERN with the phrase "… here the Web was born!"

CERN is "its own sort of United Nations of the scientific world" where 6500 scientists from 80 countries work together (<http://www.exploratorium.edu/origins/ cern/place/index.html>). The proposal was written to solve the problem of linking together different kinds of information — "reports, experiment data, personnel data, electronic mail address lists, computer documentation, experiment documentation, and many other sets of data." It proposes using a novel but simple concept of using hypertext to provide a single user interface to access different classes of information stored at remote systems using networks. The proposal is rather short but is quite specific and concrete. It includes information on concepts, applications, scope, requirements analysis, architecture, building blocks, project phases, resources required, and future work.

The reason this rather limited proposal became the beginning of the now exponentially significant World Wide Web is the simplicity of the proposal and the fact that it elegantly addressed a highly significant problem that existed in the large community of scientific and academic computer users.

Problem Selection and Development Patterns (Awareness of Problem Phase)

Problem Formulation

The problem was formulated based on the observed needs of CERN to utilize the available HyperText technology to integrate together information within the organization through a common interface, thus overcoming a major problem of not being able to look up existing information because of incompatibilities of platforms and tools. The problem was stated in a way that makes it sound like a development problem instead of a major research problem. It is the solution approach that has made the solution a major advance.

Cost-Benefit Analysis

As expected from a good proposal, it first sketches the benefits of the proposed work. The stated benefits were the ability to access information of various kinds such as reports, notes, databases, documentation, and online help, all of which had been created and stored autonomously, using a common user interface and hyperlinks. The needed resources — people (system architects, hyper-librarians, software engineers), workstations, software, computer support, office area — were then outlined. The project was divided into two phases, the first phase lasting three months and the second phase lasting six months.

Being Visionary

The proposal envisioned a radical departure from the existing environment in which data and information were not available in a timely fashion, leading to frustration, wasted time, and obsolete answers.

Literature Search Patterns (Awareness of Problem Phase)

Industry and Practice Awareness

The work obviously was strongly tied to practice and its awareness. It was motivated by the identification of productivity impediments that needed to be removed. This is a good example of a research advance that resulted from a bold attempt to solve a real problem in practice.

Suggestion and Development Patterns (Suggestion and Development Phases)

Research Community Tools and Techniques

The authors of the proposal were obviously aware of the tools and techniques used in this type of research. Prototyping was correctly selected as the appropriate technique to demonstrate the proposed concept and the feasibility of its implementation.

Empirical Refinement

The project focused on the essential aspects of the project, which was ambitious but do-able. They alluded to the fact that completion of the two phases of the project would provide "an extremely useful set of tools" that would be further enhanced in the future and would be studied for its use and abuse at CERN. Both of these observations were extremely prescient given the subsequent rise of the World Wide Web and the research and development efforts to which it gave rise.

Easy Solution First

The project attempted to implement a simple scheme that would provide a basic protocol for requesting diverse types of human-readable information stored in different types of servers on a network using HyperText to serve as a single user interface. This way the project focused on the essential idea instead of complex issues and enhancements such as the use of fancy multimedia or the use of sophisticated network authorization systems.

Elegant Design

The proposed design had all the characteristics of elegance. It was general in terms of the types of data files and the types of servers, display devices, and browsers used.

Hierarchical Design

The overall system was divided into two building blocks — browsers and servers — and how the two can be linked together. Design issues for each of the components were identified and solutions proposed.

Sketching Solution

The authors provided a succinct outline of their proposed solution within a proposal that is six pages long. The solution sketch clearly brings out the central concept of the solution as well as the areas that should be the focus of the project.

Combining Partial Solutions

The contribution of the project is not in proposing a new technology but rather the concept of a simple protocol that forms the glue for utilizing the technologies of HyperText and HTML for linking together diverse types of information on different types of servers connected through a network. HyperText is the main underlying technology used in the solution.

Evaluation and Validation Patterns (Evaluation Phase)

Demonstration

The authors proposed to demonstrate their concept through a carefully designed prototype that demonstrates the generality as well as the feasibility of its implementation. This is quite appropriate for the objectives and non-objectives listed in the proposal and in a situation where a novel concept is being proposed for the first time.

"The Entity-Relationship Model: Toward a Unified View of Data"

Source

Chen, P. (1976). The Entity-Relationship Model: Toward a Unified View of Data. *ACM Transactions on Database Systems*, 1(1), 9–37.

Problem Selection and Development Patterns (Awareness of Problem Phase)

Research Conversation

This paper revealed the author's awareness of the research conversations going on in the database community with respect to the prevailing data models and their strengths and weaknesses. The author identified a knowledge gap from an analysis of the existing literature.

Being Visionary

Chen was aware of the literature on existing data models and their strengths and limitations. The network model can provide a natural representational view of data but its capability to achieve data independence between how it is represented and its use in applications had been challenged. The relational model provides a high degree of data independence but may not capture important semantic information about the domain being modeled. The entity set model also provides a high degree of data independence but introduces a degree of artificiality by treating everything, including a value, as an entity. Chen envisioned a model that generalizes these models while modeling data at a conceptual level.

Literature Search Patterns (Awareness of Problem Phase)

Understanding Research Community

The author demonstrated a good understanding of the literature, discussing the differences between the network and the relational model as well as attempts at reducing the differences between the two models.

Framework Development

The author extended an existing framework for a deeper understanding of the existing literature. The framework contains four levels that range from the conceptual level (information existing in people's minds) to the physical level (access-path-dependent data structures).

Suggestion and Development Patterns (Suggestion and Development Phases)

Approaches for Building Theory

The theory consists of the proposed new model and shows how it relates to the existing literature. The model was developed using intuition and an understanding of the existing literature and its shortcomings in the area of data modeling.

Problem Space Tools and techniques

Chen specifically addressed the problem of modeling data at a conceptual level using graphics to represent the model.

Different Perspectives

Aided by a framework, the author was able to present a new perspective on data modeling that existing models had not addressed. This perspective was that of the conceptual modeling that is critical to understanding data and its relationships from the problem perspective.

General Solution Principle

Chen showed that his proposed new model is a generalization of existing data models. He showed that the three existing data models in the literature can be derived from the entity-relationship model.

Evaluation and Validation Patterns (Evaluation Phase)

Demonstration

Chen used parts of an example drawn from the manufacturing domain to demonstrate the new model, along with a diagrammatic technique and its use in database design. Note that this sparse level of evaluation and validation, while acceptable in 1976, would probably not be publishable today. Of course, literally hundreds of studies, elements of which would need to be incorporated into the paper if it were a contemporary development, have since been performed on this model showing its cognitive and practical utility

Publishing Patterns (Conclusion Phase)

Use of Examples

The author used parts of a running example from the manufacturing domain to illustrate the use of the new model and to enhance the readability of the paper. The example deals with entities such as Employees, Departments, Projects, Suppliers, and Parts to which the reader can easily relate.

"A Relational Model of Data for Large Shared Data Banks"

Source

Codd, E. (1970). A Relational Model of Data for Large Shared Data Banks. *Communications of the ACM*, 13(6), 377–387. Reprinted in *Communications of the ACM, 25th Anniversary Issue*, 26(1), 64–69, January 1983.

Creativity Patterns

Wild Combinations

Codd made a bold departure from conventional thinking. He saw a major gap in knowledge dealing with the problem of data independence — independence between the use of data in application programs and its representation in data banks — and in proposing a solution that uses relational theory and predicate calculus.

Problem Selection and Development Patterns (Awareness of Problem Phase)

Research Conversation

Codd demonstrated a good understanding of the existing research in the area. He recognized that in the database systems being developed, the data representation characteristics could not be changed without impairing some application program. He also realized that the existing data models were cluttered with physical representational properties such as ordering, indexing, and access path dependencies.

Solution and Scope Mismatch

Codd realized that the database systems using the existing data models — network and hierarchical models — were able to support application programs but only as long as the stored data characteristics were not changed or the structure of the files used in storing the data was not changed. This gave rise to the research problem of handling data independence and consistency.

Being Visionary

Codd analyzed the existing models, network and hierarchical, for representing data and envisioned a solution that would address the problem of data dependence and inconsistency. The knowledge gap between the existing situation and the envisioned situation was identified as the research problem.

Questioning Constraints

Codd questioned the constraint imposed by the database research community of not making a distinction between the logical view of data and its physical representation. This, he claimed, opens up degrees of freedom for how data can be logically represented.

Literature Search Patterns (Awareness of Problem Phase)

Industry and Practice Awareness

Codd was working at IBM and was keenly aware of the existing database management systems and their limitations.

Suggestion and Development Patterns (Suggestion and Development Phases)

Approaches to Building Theory

Codd used the hypothetical and deductive approach to theory development. He critically reviewed the network and hierarchical models, and used intuition and his extensive background in mathematical modeling to develop the relational model and its associated theory.

Elegant Design

Codd created an artifact, the relational model, which can be functionally described as supporting data independence and consistency instead of the details of its construction. The artifact therefore has the characteristics of elegant design.

Different Perspectives

Codd provided a different perspective on data modeling by making a distinction between physical data modeling and logical data modeling, the latter being at a higher level of abstraction.

Evaluation and Validation Patterns (Evaluation Phase)

Demonstration

Codd did not develop a prototype because the goal was to demonstrate the new concepts that he proposed at a theoretical level. Instead, he used the example of a data bank containing data about parts, projects, and suppliers to demonstrate that the solution proposed is realizable and valid.

Publishing Patterns (Conclusion Phase)

Novelty and Significance

Codd wrote this paper in such a way as to clearly show the novelty and significance of his research. In the introduction of the paper, he positioned his research with respect to prior research on data modeling and showed a gap in the existing knowledge on data independence. He also showed the significance of his work in the concluding section of the paper where he stated the many questions raised in the paper but left unanswered, such as the linguistic details of the needed data languages and their implementation.

Use of Examples

Codd used an elaborate example of a data bank (base) containing data about parts, projects, and suppliers to illustrate how the relational model can be used and to demonstrate how the model achieves data independence. The example makes the paper better understandable and also convinces the reader about the significance of the research.

"The Working Set Model for Program Behavior"

Source

Denning, P. (1968). The Working Set Model for Program Behavior. *Communications of the ACM*, 11(5), 323–333. Reprinted in *Communications of the ACM, 25th Anniversary Issue*, 26(1), 43–48, January 1983.

Problem Selection and Development Patterns (Awareness of Problem Phase)

Research Conversation

Denning analyzed the research conversations going on in the operating systems community through conference and journal papers. He found that the research allocation problem for multi-programmed computers (in which multiple programs execute at the same time) had progressed independently for allocating core memory and for process scheduling. He reasoned that the absence of a general treatment of resource allocation is due to a "lack of an adequate model for program behavior" and then proceeded to fill this knowledge gap.

Solution and Scope Mismatch

Denning analyzed a number of existing memory management algorithms and found that while they worked well in particular constrained situations, they did not do as well in the general situation. For example, the first-in/first-out strategy works well when the programs exhibit a sequential instruction fetch pattern. Similarly, the least-recently-used page selection strategy works well in a single-process situation but not in a multi-process situation. He set out to address the problem in the most general situation.

Being Visionary

Denning envisioned an approach in which the management of system resources — memory allocation, and process and process scheduling — is addressed through a uniform approach in which the operating system balances processor and memory demands against available resources based on an analysis of program behavior.

Literature Search Patterns (Awareness of Problem Phase)

Understanding Research Community

Denning developed his research problem based on an in-depth understanding and analysis of the operating systems research community. He also credited the working set concept to a number of reports associated with the pioneering research performed at MIT under the auspices of Project MAC.

Suggestion and Development Patterns (Suggestion and Development Phases)

Elegant Design

The central concept of the working set model is the working set of pages associated with a process, defined as the collection of its most recently used pages. The model is general and can be described in terms of its properties.

Different Perspectives

Denning, while understanding and building on the existing literature, provided a different perspective on what should be done to solve the problem. He initiated an analytical approach for examining the properties of the proposed working set model. He also showed that a computation's processor demand and its memory demand in a multi-programmed environment (where multiple programs are executing at the same time) are the manifestations of the same ongoing computation activity.

General Solution Principle

Denning developed a number of basic properties that must hold for resource allocation in computer systems and also developed the working set model as an approach for solving the problem. He then expanded on this work to show that the model can be used for balancing the processor and memory demands of a program.

Evaluation and Validation Pattern (Evaluation Phase)

Logical Reasoning

Denning used logical arguments to show the weaknesses of the existing solutions, to show the reasonableness of the assumptions he made, and to show how the working set model can be useful as a basis for memory management.

Publishing Patterns (Conclusion Phase)

Novelty and Significance

Denning wrote this paper in such a way as to clearly show the novelty and significance of his research. In the "Introduction" section, he positioned his research with respect to prior research on memory management by showing the gap in existing knowledge to be the lack of a unified approach to balancing memory and processor demand. Denning also positioned his research as commencement of a stream of research on resources based on the working set model.

"Communicating Sequential Processes"

Source

Hoare, C. (1978). Communicating Sequential Processes. *Communications of the ACM,* 21(8), 666–677. Reprinted in *Communications of the ACM, 25th Anniversary Issue,* 26(1), 100–106, January 1983.

Problem Selection and Development Patterns (Awareness of Problem Phase)

Research Conversation

Hoare demonstrated his awareness of the literature on computer programming and high-level programming languages. He cited literature for methods that have been suggested for using a multiprocessor computer to execute a single task effectively. He proposed to synthesize the available literature into a simple solution.

Abstraction

Hoare abstracted the problem of effectively using a multiprocessor machine for executing a single task to that of finding a few abstract concepts that should underlie the design of a programming language used for the purpose. He suggested input, output, and concurrency (parallel composition of communicating sequential processes) as fundamental abstract concepts that should underlie any programming language for writing programs that effectively use a multiprocessor machine.

Suggestion and Development Patterns (Suggestion and Development Phases)

Elegant Design

Hoare designed a simple programming language with a few primitive concepts that can be used for writing any program that effectively uses parallel processing.

Note that parsimony of constructs is a general research principle (cf. Occam's razor) across *all* research methods. It leads to elegant empirical research designs as well as strong and elegant design research contributions.

General Solution Principle

Hoare showed the generality of his proposed language, CSP (Communicating Sequential Processes), by demonstrating that constructs such as monitors and procedures, and solutions to famous programming problems such as the Dining Philosophers problem, can be modeled using CSP.

Integrating Techniques

The CSP language adapts and integrates available concepts in the existing literature, such as Dijkstra's guarded command and parbegin.

Evaluation and Validation Patterns (Evaluation Phase)

Demonstration

Hoare demonstrated the versatility and generality of CSP by demonstrating how CSP can be used to express solutions to many programming problems that have previously been used in the literature to illustrate the use of various programming language features.

Logical Reasoning

Hoare provided clear reasoning for the motivation of CSP and why a few underlying primitive concepts of CSP are enough to model the many elaborate constructs that were being used in programming languages.

Publishing Patterns (Conclusion Phase)

Aligning with a Paradigm

The work is clearly positioned in the programming and programming languages literature with respect to shared symbols and beliefs of the research community. It uses the well-accepted Backus-Naur Form (BNF) notation for specifying CSP and builds on the published work of Dijkstra.

Novelty and Significance

Hoare examined the existing programming literature to show that the operations of input and output were not well understood in a formal sense. He also showed the lack of agreement in choosing among different available solutions for expressing a program that can be effectively run on a multiprocessor machine. He then proposed a simple solution, CSP. The paper thus clearly showed the novelty and significance of its contribution.

Use of Examples

The paper used a number of well-known examples such as the Dining Philosophers problem to make the paper more readable, as well as to demonstrate its contribution (cf. the use of the "grocery bagging" example to illustrate and validate the smart object paradigm, "An Example of ICT Design Science Research" in Chapter 2).

"Optimum Multiway Search Trees"

Source

Vaishnavi, V., Kriegel, H., and Wood, D. (1980). Optimum Multiway Search Trees. *Acta Informatica*, 14, 119–133.

Problem Selection and Development Patterns (Awareness of Problem Phase)

Research Conversation

An analysis of the literature revealed that while an efficient algorithm existed for constructing optimal binary search trees, there did not exist any such algorithm for constructing multiway search trees that are used for storing data on secondary storage. The resulting literature fit well with the then-ongoing research conversations in the area.

Solution and Scope Mismatch

Knuth (D.E. Knuth, Optimum Binary Search Trees, *Acta Informatica*, 1, 14–25, 1971) published an $O(n^2)$ time solution for constructing optimal binary search trees. This was the only polynomial time algorithm for the problem and was a reasonably good solution. However, binary search trees are useful for storing data only in *primary storage*; they are not useful when the data is very large and must be stored in secondary storage (such as disk storage). For disk storage, one should use a k-ary search tree, $k \geq 3$, with the value of k depending on disk page size and other considerations. Thus, the efficient construction of an optimal k-ary search tree was an interesting research problem.

The problem had not been addressed in the literature. Instead of trying a new solution technique, Vaishnavi et al. considered a straightforward application of the dynamic programming solution technique proposed by Knuth. This approach led to an $O(n^{k+1})$ algorithm with a possible improvement to $O(n^k)$. This was not a feasible solution because k can be as large as 500. This gave rise to a research problem that was important and for which simple extension of an existing technique did not lead to a reasonable solution. Before trying a completely different technique, an attempt was made to apply the dynamic programming technique in a different manner. An optimality principle was discovered that was not a simple generalization of the corresponding principle for the binary search tree case. This gave rise to a reasonable algorithm that could also be "tuned" to other such problems with additional constraints.

Solution and Theory Development Patterns (Suggestion and Development Phases)

Modeling Existing Solutions

An existing solution for binary search trees based on dynamic programming was modeled and then modified to develop the solution for the corresponding problem for multiway search trees.

General Solution Principle

A number of basic results that must hold for any optimal multiway search tree were first developed. The authors then identified the dynamic programming technique as an approach for constructing optimal search trees with a number of different additional constraints. Using the general basic results, they developed an optimality principle that could be integrated into the dynamic programming technique to result in a general solution for the given class of problems. They finally tuned the solution to a number of specific instances of the class of problems to improve their solutions.

Evaluation and Validation Patterns (Evaluation Phase)

Using Metrics

The authors analyzed their proposed algorithm and proved that an optimal k-ary search tree can be constructed in $O(n^3 k)$ time, which can be reduced to $O(n^2 k)$

time for a special case of the problem. There was no previously published solution to the problem, and the solution provided by the authors had a reasonable polynomial time performance. This showed that the solution was reasonably efficient.

Mathematical Proofs

In this paper, the authors proved that the proposed algorithm would indeed construct an *optimal* multiway search tree. They also proved the claimed time-complexity of the proposed algorithm.

Publishing Patterns (Conclusion Phase)

Style Exemplars

The work was motivated by a 1972 paper by Knuth published in *Acta Informatica*. Knuth gave an efficient algorithm for constructing optimal binary search trees, which are useful for organizing data in the primary storage. The authors posed a similar problem for multiway search trees, which are used for organizing data in the secondary storage. Knuth was well regarded in the field. The authors chose to write their paper for *Acta Informatica* and used Knuth's paper as a style exemplar for writing the paper. The paper was accepted without any revision.

Novelty and Significance

The authors develop their research problem in the context of the existing literature, showing its novelty and importance. They differentiate the problem of constructing an optimal multiway search tree from that of constructing an optimal binary search tree and discuss the importance of the former problem. They also discuss why an efficient algorithm for the problem does not follow from any existing work, including that of Knuth's work for constructing an optimal binary search tree.

Index